For my father, who believed in simplicity

The Money Well

HOW TO CONTAIN WEALTH

KIKI THEO

ILLUSTRATIONS BY
SIMONE REDMAN

PENGUIN BOOKS

PENGUIN BOOKS

Published by the Penguin Group
Penguin Books (South Africa) (Pty) Ltd, 24 Sturdee Avenue, Rosebank, Johannesburg 2196, South Africa
Penguin Group (USA) Inc, 375 Hudson Street, New York, New York 10014, USA
Penguin Group (Canada), 90 Eglinton Avenue East, Suite 700, Toronto, Ontario, Canada M4P 2Y3 (a division of Pearson Penguin Canada Inc)
Penguin Books Ltd, 80 Strand, London WC2R 0RL, England
Penguin Ireland, 25 St Stephen's Green, Dublin 2, Ireland (a division of Penguin Books Ltd)
Penguin Group (Australia), 250 Camberwell Road, Camberwell, Victoria 3124, Australia (a division of Pearson Australia Group Pty Ltd)
Penguin Books India Pvt Ltd, 11 Community Centre, Panchsheel Park, New Delhi – 110 017, India
Penguin Group (NZ), 67 Apollo Dŕ
division of Pearson New Zealand Ltc

Penguin Books (South Africa) (Pty)
24 Sturdee Avenue, Rosebank, Johar

www.penguinbooks.co.za

First published by Penguin Books (S

Copyright © Kyriaki Theodosiadis 2

Contents

Part I: Containing Wealth

Part II: How to Clear Obstacles to Wealth: Transforming Leaks and Blocks to Wealth Flow and Wealth Containment

Chapter 1 The Flow

Chapter 2 Belief Systems

Chapter 3 Attitude

Part I

Containing Wealth

1

In the Beginning

Why are you reading this book? What do you want to achieve?

The Well and the Bucket full of Holes
A tale

Once upon a time, in a land far, far away, there lived a little girl. She loved to dress up in beautiful clothes and she absolutely loved jewels! Her favourite possession was a shiny silver tiara decorated with sequins and rhinestones which she wore with a golden dress and her mother's high-heeled shoes. Then she would strike a pose in front of her red plastic mirror and imagine herself stepping out of a long silver limousine. Holding her head up high, she would turn this way and that, nodding at her imaginary audience as she swept regally by, swaying her little hips just so. She was not quite sure where this scene would take place – all she knew was that she would be there! She would be rich and famous. She would be a movie star!

The little girl grew up strong and beautiful, but life was hard, and over time she stopped dressing up. She often daydreamed. But always her mother's call brought her back to the village and to her many chores.

Every day, wearing her homespun dress, the young girl walked barefoot towards the well for the daily ritual of gathering water. The well was ancient, deep, and filled with dark cool water. The well represented life in the village, for without water the crops could not grow, the animals would die and so would the villagers.

The wealthy villagers, those who would soon leave for the cities, were the ones with their own stores of water – water which they could use to cultivate more land and cool more animals. They were the lucky ones, her mother said, born under a lucky moon. You could not fight the fates. They were either for you or against you. Hard work was the only thing you could depend on. The rest was just foolish dreams, so said the young girl's mother.

With a deep sigh, the young girl began her daily ritual of drawing water and carrying it home, a process she would repeat over and over again until the small stone dam outside their kitchen door was full. It was a gruelling process, for her bucket leaked, and once she had filled it she had to run as fast as her legs could carry her to reach home before all the water was lost for ever. Still, she managed to hold on to a little water on each trip, and in this way slowly, slowly, she filled up the dam. But there was never, ever, enough for more. And as time went by the young girl forgot her dreams. She lost the sparkle in her step and in her eyes, and she focused all her efforts on trying to fill the small dam using the leaking bucket . . . (*to be continued*)

Filling up the holes

'It's not how much money you get to make, it's how much money you get to keep, that's the issue,' Oprah has said. And that is exactly the subject of this book. For, very much like the girl in the story, we go to the well of plenty with a bucket full of holes, and wonder why we cannot have the plenty.

The Money Well™ deals with how to contain money and its flow. Part One sets the groundwork for the next section, which addresses how to discover and deal with obstructions to the flow and containment of wealth. *The Money Well*™ works with the metaphor of a container. The container is your vision, your destination and your goal. But, mostly, your container is the quest for a new wealthy you. *The Money Well*™ looks at your wealth container in terms of its make-up – its size, shape, material, base and opening; what will cause it to become full or empty; and how to prevent leaks. In *The Money Well*™ you are guided to reflect on how money, and your life in general, flows and how you contain.

The Money Well™ will enable you to create a container that can truly accommodate you and your wealth. It will help you to let go of and transform anything which is not in alignment with your wealth creation path. *The Money Well*™ will help you to uncover and build the container of your vision, your dreams and your new wealthy self. Furthermore, the powerful processing in *The Money Well*™ which uses a combination of symbol, visualisation and energetic transformation, with intent, will clear and open up the flow of wealth towards you.

This work will transform you – organically, subtly, and powerfully – into someone who can contain more – more money, more wealth, more life, more you!

To contain more, you must become more
Kiki Theo

Looking backwards and forwards

Many of you have read *Money Alchemy – into wealth and beyond*. (If you haven't, get a copy.) *The Money Well*™ begins with a slightly modified version of a chapter from the *Money Alchemy* book entitled 'Money as Potential'. Although *The Money Well*™ follows on from *Money Alchemy*, where the money journey began, it is also a self-contained (ha, ha) book which can be used without having read the first one. *The Money Well*™ is about wealth expansion.

Instructions on how to use the book and an explanation of the wealth processing techniques it describes are given at the end of the book (page 252), together with a bit of my story. Read that first. Then you can jump straight in. You need not interrupt your reading to do the processing. Read *The Money Well*™ through first, to get the gist of it. Then begin the processing, slowly, methodically, with the right intent and with lightness, excitement and fun. You are learning how to contain the universe! How cool is that?

Approach this wealth expansion journey like a quest. The very nature of the subject is the transformation of shadow – those aspects of our nature which will yield the light. With this intent we dip deep into the well of our own consciousness, the well of true wealth, and seek its treasures.

- What is *your* intent? Why are you reading this book? What do you hope to achieve, learn, transform?
- What are you hoping to contain or expand?
- Stating your intent, clearly (and with intent . . .) will greatly enhance the wins you derive from reading this book.
- Decide now that this book will act as catalyst to transform your life completely, taking you to the next level.
- State your intent HERE! 'It is my intent that reading this book will . . .'
- (Don't be shy, reach for the stars!)

Here is my intent for this book:
> *It is my intent that this book will reach millions of people around the globe.*
> *May every reader unite and support the intent to expand, flourish, and prosper for the greatest good of all!*
> *May we join together to create a global container for peace, wealth and happiness.*
>
> Kiki Theo, February 2009

I wish you luck on this, the next part of your money journey!

Let the journey begin! Good Luck!

> *It's good to have money and the things money can buy,*
> *but it's good, too, to check up once in a while and be sure*
> *you haven't lost the things money can't buy*
>
> George Horace Lorimer

2

Containing Wealth

If you had all the money in the world, where would you contain it?

In this chapter, which is a slightly amended version of a chapter in the *Money Alchemy* book, we will review the key aspects of a container and containment. We will then go into each aspect in depth in the chapters that follow.

It will grow as big as the pot

Bonsai is the art of stunting the growth of trees by regularly clipping the roots and branches. A miniature fig tree, for example, is kept tiny by being contained in a small, shallow, ornamental pot. The seed of the fig tree has the potential to grow to a height of 30 metres (100 feet), but when it is not given a large enough container to expand in, it cannot fulfil its potential.

Goldfish will grow according to the size of the pond or fish tank they are in. The bigger the container, the larger they grow, and vice versa. Strangely enough, this also applies to crocodiles – and to money.

Money is sheer potential. It can become anything you want it to be. It is amorphous, diaphanous, invisible – it is energy, all around us, but unseen. Like the wind, it is a powerful force when concentrated. Like energy, it can do amazing things when mobilised. Money is not a static. It is not an object, or even a means to an end. It is not something you go and fetch, or acquire.

Money is potential, and it needs containment. Money needs to find form. This is what we offer money. Without form, money cannot exist, nor can it fulfil itself as potential. You may find this way of looking at money rather strange, but think of this:

> *Only the most foolish of mice would hide in a cat's ear.*
> *But only the wisest of cats would think to look there*
> Scott Love

That's called, in this context, a *koan* (which has various spellings) – a way of short circuiting the mind so it can give you a break while it tries to figure out what this means!

The point is, you cannot hold on to money, you can only contain it, and in order to contain money, you need a container.

> *We know what we are, not what we may become*
> William Shakespeare

Go with the flow!

Unless we create a container for money to flow into, where is it going to go? How will it translate itself from potential into reality? How will it take form? Money is an energy, a flow, a force, certainly something that is in motion, and in the process of becoming – it needs to be harnessed and contained or we might find ourselves thinking it's not really there. (This is called the mentality of lack.)

How we contain money is reflected in how we contain other things in our lives – our dreams, hopes, and aspirations, our goals, our relationships, our vision, our humanity, our weight. Ultimately, how we contain money reflects our ability to have. And as our ability to have arises out of our ability to be, or who we are, we can say that how we contain money is how we contain our beingness. Our beingness is limitless, we have unlimited potential but we need to find it, direct it, and contain it. I wrote the following parable to illustrate this point.

The Earthenware Bowl and the River of Gold
A tale

There once lived a man of modest means. He was hard working and good and he lived in a lovely house in the forest. His house was surrounded by a wall, which had an opening on the east side. Every morning, before the sun came up, gold would flow from the opening in the wall into a small earthenware bowl that the man placed there every evening.

The man used the gold to buy seeds and to grow vegetables and fruit. He bought corn and he made butter and cheese. He mended his house when this was needed and he tended his garden. He lived a simple life, but there was never time to rest or to enjoy the beautiful sunsets. He longed for a wife and a family. He yearned to see the world beyond the walls of his house.

But his work was long and hard and every evening, quite exhausted, he carefully washed his small earthenware bowl and put it out at the opening on the east side of the wall, and went to sleep.

The bowl had been given to him by his father, who had been given it by his father before him.

'Look after this bowl, my son, for this is your livelihood. As long as you take care of this bowl, you will never go hungry,' his father had said.

'It's a little small, Dad,' he had answered. 'I could make a new one, bigger, stronger, perhaps with a bold design.'

But his father had mocked the idea.

'Sheer foolishness, my boy, wild dreams!' he'd said. 'Stick with what works.'

And so it was that the river of gold that flowed just outside the house rose with the tides every evening and poured through the opening in the east side of the wall. It filled the little earthenware bowl many times over, the excess spilling out over the sides for many hours, to be absorbed back into the earth. When daylight came, the tide receded, leaving the little earthenware bowl full of gold. Just full enough to fill the bowl, and just enough gold to meet the man's needs.

Find the river or widen the bowl?

That's really the question – not how come the man in the story did not see the river, or why it was rising at night, or why it was full of gold. This is a parable, after all!

We often try to find the river of gold. That's what we try to do when we go to the casino, or play the lottery. Sometimes our company gets bought for a large sum of money, or our invention is snapped up by the Danish (or the Chinese), or we inherit from that uncle who was reputed to have been a pirate. And, lo and behold, we have found the river of gold!

Interestingly enough, most (though not all) of the people who suddenly acquire large sums of money, quite rapidly revert to where they were before the gain. There is extensive research on this phenomenon.

Who can direct the flow of the river?

Why is this so? Quite simply, it's the inability to contain. Finding the river is not enough. For unless we can direct the flow of the river towards a destination, unless we can contain it, the river will continue to flow past us unseen. This is the river of money we are talking about.

This is the river of unmanifest potential, pure energy, which is everywhere around us, waiting to find form, yearning to be contained and so made visible.

By directing the river, we help it to fulfil its potential, we direct it towards its goal. And once it arrives there safely, we contain this river of potential, of money, of dreams, of our unmanifest magnificence, in a wonderful expansive, magnificent container. And when we successfully do this, we realise that it is we who have journeyed along the river, it is we who have arrived at the destination, in fact it is we who are both the river and the container.

You must broaden your girth

As for the container, it definitely needs to be large enough to contain our goal, it must also be built sturdily and have no leaks. It must be expandable, and easily accessed by the river. For if your money container is not large enough, you will find that no matter how much you earn, you will always be in the same place in the wealth department.

You may have had this experience already. Suddenly there is a windfall of some kind, or an increase in income, and then you find something needs repairing, or an unpaid bill emerges. Why? It is because you have not adjusted the size of your container to contain more. So the excess merely flows away. To contain more money, you need a bigger container. It's actually quite simple.

What do you Contain?
Wealth Training Process

The exercises that follow will help you to focus on the metaphor of container from many different angles. You will draw your container and write about it, you will also reflect upon its size, shape, balance, support and base. Using prompts, you will reflect on aspects of containment within your life using free writing as a tool. You will be asking yourself questions like, 'How do I contain my life, gifts, talents?'; 'How does my money contain me?'; 'What do my beliefs *not* contain?' Begin by reviewing the instructions on how to do the processing at the end of the book.

If you are not able to do the processing now, skip to the next section, and come back to this later. But do come back! The successful transformation of your wealth container depends on doing *the processing!*

Allow yourself to learn about yourself through these exercises. Permit yourself to reveal layers below the surface. Know that this new knowledge is yours to keep. You need not share it with anyone. No one is watching you write. No one will read what you write. Let rip!

Before you start, STATE YOUR INTENT! Be clear and specific. For example:
> *'It is my intent that this processing will release the flow of wealth in my life and I am able to contain it.'*

Keep your pen moving
Write/draw without thinking
Repeat the prompt if you are stuck
Keep it light!

Drawing your Container
Wealth Training Process

- Set aside ten minutes for this exercise.
- Get a large piece of blank paper (A4 or bigger) and a box of crayons, or coloured pencils.
- Label the paper 'My Container'.
- For three minutes draw your container – don't think about this. Allow what emerges to emerge. Use colour boldly or draw with fine pencil strokes – whatever you feel best suits your container.
- Jot down as quickly as you can five words or short phrases that came into your mind as you drew.
- Then, looking at your drawing, write about it for five minutes.
- Underline important words or phrases and summarise these into one sentence.
- Turn the picture upside down.
- Write about what you see now – don't think about it.
- Once again, underline important words or phrases and summarise these into a sentence.
- Observe your container without judgement:
  - > Is it big or small?
  - > Tall or short?
  - > Wide or narrow?
  - > What is it made of?
  - > Are the walls thick or thin?
  - > Does it have a firm base?
  - > Is it supported?
  - > What supports it?
  - > Is the opening at the top wide or narrow?
  - > Does it leak?
  - > Is it full or empty?

11

> Is it overflowing?
> What is around the container? That is, how is the container contained?

Underline important words or phrases and summarise everything into one sentence.

You will be re-examining and possibly adjusting this container throughout this book, so keep this drawing handy.

How Do I Contain Various Aspects of My Life?
Wealth Training Process

(a) Using the prompts below, write for two minutes on each one individually: (Keep your hand moving, repeat the prompt if you get stuck.)

- I contain ....   I do not contain ....
- My body contains ....   My body does not contain ....
- My beliefs contain ....   My beliefs do not contain ....
- My thinking contains ....   My thinking does not contain ....
- My talents contain ....   My talents do not contain ....
- My skills contain ....   My skills do not contain ....
- My views contain ....   My views do not contain ....
- My heart contains ....   My heart does not contain ....
- My wealth contains ....   My wealth does not contain ....
- My truth contains ....   My truth does not contain ....
- My being contains ....   My being does not contain ....
- My relationships contain .....   My relationships do not contain ....
- My work contains ....   My work does not contain ....

Take a short break and move around

Now, using the prompts below, write for two minutes on each one individually:
(Keep your hand moving, repeat the prompt if you get stuck.)
- My dreams contain ....   My dreams do not contain ....
- My goals contain ....   My goals do not contain ....
- My money contains ....   My money does not contain ....

- My debt contains ....   My debt does not contain ....
- My vision contains ....   My vision does not contain ....
- My life contains ....   My life does not contain ....
- My potential contains ....   My potential does not contain ....
- My expectations contain .... My expectations do not contain ....
- My destination contains .... My destination does not contain ....

Underline important words or phrases and summarise everything into one sentence.

(b) Do all of the above prompts, switched around to read:
- I contain my body ....   I do not contain my body..........
- I contain my beliefs..........   I do not contain my beliefs..........

and so on.

Underline important words or phrases and summarise everything into one sentence.

(c) Summarise the entire exercise (a and b) into ONE sentence. What does all that mean to you?
(d) Record any decisions you want to take and any inspired actions you want to perform as a result of these reflections. Well done!
(e) Now execute your decisions and actions.

Free writing from prompts will become easier as you go along, but in case you've never tried this before, here's an example of a two-minute free write based on one of the points above, written by a friend. (Of course, if you've read and done the work in *Money Alchemy*, you'll be an old hand at timed free writing!)

> ***My views contain*** *everything I have seen and have yet to see, heard and have yet to hear, experienced and have yet to experience. Even if I think I have rejected or discarded some of these, they are still here, will arrive here, in me, leaving their imprint on my ways of looking, they are what has shaped my way of seeing, being and reacting. And I know there are 13*

*ways of looking at a blackbird and 13.13.13 ways of looking
at my world, but . . . My world. What I see and am in it
makes my views. So I'm not sure about how to write the next
prompt – what my views do not contain. I contain all that has
happened to me.*

*So how do I write about what **my views do** not **contain**? I
find it easier to be specific than I thought. My views do not
contain misogyny or bigotry or chauvinism or cruelty. I like
to think that my views are open (minded) enough to respect
other points of view. But that doesn't mean I have to absorb
or integrate these into my world view. And so the list grows
. . . I cannot bear to think of containing an opinion or point
of view that allows abuse of any kind, to any living creature.
More thoughts, faster than I can write – I'm cooking ideas
under pressure realising – adamantly – that experience shapes
me in two ways – it shapes what I want to be and hold as
views or opinions and it also allows me to reject the unaccept-
able. Phew – buzzer!*

What have you accomplished?

In this process you reflected on 'you' as a container of things and
you examined how you contain various aspects of your life. You
also contemplated how various aspects of your life contain you.
You are beginning to consider money as something you need to
contain, and you are reviewing the ways in which you have contained money up until this point. You are embracing the concept
of creating a container for your money, and are considering the
possibilities for this version of reality.

This new thinking energy will form new patterns, which will
raise new questions in your mind over the next while. Be open to
this. A pebble has been dropped into the pond of your consciousness. The journey has begun. *Well done!*

Mirror, mirror on the wall!

The most important part of any of this processing is reflection at the end. Reflecting is allowing the information to wash over you. You just observe what is. You look at what is there, with an open and enquiring attitude, ready to discover something new, ready to be surprised. Simply look and see what is there, like looking at the sunset.

Drinking from an empty cup

So, to recap. To contain something, we need a container. The container for our money is our goal or vision. Without this, we cannot hold on to (or rather, contain) our money. The container has to be durable, expandable and have no leaks. Though our container will change over time as we grow and develop, at any one moment in time, our container must have a constant and definite shape. This is very important. A half cup, half plate, maybe a tumbler will keep spilling its contents, whereas a big spaghetti pot will not. Italians will be happy to hear this.

This means that we need to have a specific goal or vision, for it is this that will contain our wealth. It is our goal that we direct our energy and intention towards. Committing to a specific goal is not easy, as we do not always know what we want. But what we want is always linked to a feeling. More on this later.

Having a specific goal creates internal tension. It commits us to a course of action, puts us on the line, presents the possibility of failure, creates the possibility for expansion, and puts up parameters of exclusion (that is, if *this* is my goal, then *that*, and *that*, is not) – all of which is challenging.

I'm not sure it's a cup, maybe it's a saucer

We generally try to avoid specifics. We try to avoid looking at our heart's desire, and instead opt for generalisations like wanting to make a lot of money, or to be comfortable. But because these generalisations have no *form*, they cannot successfully contain money, and money seldom flows towards or into them.

Your specific goal, cause, desire, destination, is what will reformulate money from mere potential into reality. Your specific goal is what will give money form, enabling it to be contained. Without a goal, without form, money remains an intangible possibility, a potential without means of actualisation. *You* are the vehicle through which money can manifest.

A saucer? But it's got handles

So let's look at this container a little more closely. What makes a container is, firstly, the walls that differentiate the inside from the outside. Without those walls we would have a plate (or something). The walls refer to parameters, boundaries, restrictions. This is a tetchy subject, without a doubt.

We are looking at a container with walls thick enough to retain the contents, with walls that will not crumble under pressure. We want sturdy walls that are at the same time flexible. They must be flexible enough to change shape when we need to create something new. They must be flexible enough to expand without breaking or leaking. The strength of your walls also represents the sincerity of your intent and of your purpose.

How strong are your boundaries? What are your parameters? What do these questions mean to you in relation to money? These are very broad questions, which will reveal fascinating information to you about your life as well as your new money container metaphor. We will deal with these aspects individually throughout this book.

I don't want that! *This* is what I want!

The walls of your container are created through choice. That is to say, your choice of destination. It is the choice of container as goal. It is the decision to pursue *this* goal. It is a definite move away from 'making lots of money', 'being comfortable' or 'having enough'. It is the moment when you say *THIS* IS WHAT I WANT! Not that, not this, but *THIS*. Have you ever noticed how direct and specific children are? They say 'I want *this* biscuit.' And they are never put off their course, no matter what. They will continue to demand the biscuit until they get it. They will not compromise.

The walls of your money container represent a decision and a selection, with no compromise. This is your goal, with full sensa-round colour and feeling.

In the second instance, the walls represent the principle of exclusion and inclusion. What will you have in your container, and what will be outside? What forms part of your new reality with money? What do you want? And, most importantly, what will you leave behind?

The thickness of the walls represents your boundaries with the world. Your own personal space boundaries. How you interact with others and how you allow them to interact with you. If the walls are too thin they will not stand. If they are too thick, nothing will come through, and it will be difficult to make changes as you develop.

Why did the chicken cross the line?

Parameters and restrictions also relate to your principles, ethics, code of honour. Literally, we are looking at which lines you are prepared to cross to reach your new horizons. We will be processing around these points in the chapter on parameters and boundaries. It is really useful to know these things, for then you need never fear having to sell your soul to the devil in order to achieve your aims. It is unnecessary to do so.

You can make money as honestly or as dishonestly as you like – you really do have that choice. Money itself is amoral (that's not the same as immoral – look it up), you are the one with higher consciousness, you are the one with choice and free will. You can make a choice about how you want to make money and what you are and are not prepared to compromise to do so. You have both the right, and the ability to do this. Exercise it.

This changes everything!

When you work with the concept of a container you will soon discover that how you contain money is reflected in how you contain other things in your life, and vice versa. How do you, and more importantly, *do you*, contain your enthusiasm, your joy, your fun, your laughter, your creativity, for example? Do you contain your dreams? Do you contain your potential?

To contain money is to contain magic. The magic is not in figures, or budgets, or retirement plans – if it was, would you be reading this book? The magic of money lies in creation, in fulfilling dreams, in connecting with your potential and finding a way to contain it and to manifest it.

Money is sheer potential, just like you. Can you catch the wind? Can you capture the starlight? Yes and no. You need to acknowledge they are there. Then, you need to create a really beautiful container. A container which is so alluring, so captivating, that the wind, or the starlight, or the money is drawn to occupy it. A truly magnificent container will beg to be filled.

Find your container. Build it beautifully, in magnificent detail. Make the walls firm and strong, but supple. Infuse your container with all the joy and thrill and wonder of finding yourself standing before it, full and overflowing. Then sit back and relax, as the pathway towards your destination unfolds, almost effortlessly. This is what we will be working towards in this book. This is what containing wealth is all about.

Far away, there in the sunshine, are my highest aspirations.
I may not reach them, but I can look up and see their beauty,
believe in them, and try to follow where they lead
Louisa May Alcott

Finding out what we want is a lifetime mission. The reflections below will help you get started. Using writing and daydreaming you will begin the journey to uncovering your heart's longing. Do this lightly, with the right intent, and with a big open ear. Listen to the quiet inner voice as it responds to these questions over the next few months. Look out for signs, dreams and clues. *Listen to the quiet inner voice.*

If you are not able to do the processing now, skip to the next section, and come back to this later. But do come back! The successful transformation of your wealth container depends on doing *the processing!*

Before you start, STATE YOUR INTENT! Be clear and specific. For example:

> **'It is my intent that this processing will release the flow of wealth in my life and I am able to contain it.'**

Keep your pen moving
Write without thinking
Repeat the prompt if you are stuck
Keep it light!

Wealth Reflections on My Container
Wealth Training Process

Write about, reflect upon, contemplate the following:
- If you had all the money in the world, what would you like to do?
- And then what would you have? (Continue asking this seven times)
- What is your earliest memory of your ideal future/profession?
- What do you really, really want to do, really?
- If you had a container, what would it be?
- What would you have inside and outside your container?
- What is your container made of?
- What is your potential? How do you contain it?
- What is your dream? How do you contain it?
- Make a wish list of everything you want. Be specific. Don't be shy.
- What do you really want?

Daydreaming in this way is the best way to get the wealth flow open.

> *Cherish every wish in your heart, however trivial it may seem.*
> *One day these trivial wishes will lead you to God*
> Deepak Chopra from *The Way of the Wizard*

19

Containing Wealth in Summary

- Money is unformed energy and potential
- Potential needs direction, form, and containment
- Your goal is your money destination
- To contain money you need a container
- Your goal is your container
- Your money container must be specific
- Your container represents your choice of destination or goal
- The container walls represent boundaries and parameters
- The container walls must be strong, yet flexible
- Money will be drawn to fill your container
- You must expand your container as your money needs expand
- You contain the money
- You contain many aspects of your life
- Your ability to contain will determine what is contained
- Your ability to contain reflects your ability to be
- You must increase your beingness to increase your container
- You are your money container
- You are the potential unfolding

3

Your Container

Is your container big enough to hold the future you?

The Money Container

First of all, you must have a container. I cannot stress this point enough. Unless you have a container you will be unable to contain money. Even if money flows around you in torrents (which it actually does, unseen, all day long, as money is energy, and energy is everywhere), you will be unable to do anything with it if you do not have a container.

You can only hold on to so much, and then you need to contain. Holding on to anything is hard. Be it a marriage, a job, a position, an illusion, a thought, or money. It's a little like the monkey with the hand in the jar grasping a handful of nuts. Once the hand is full you can neither remove the hand, nor grasp more. Holding on, grasping, does not work. Or rather it works in a very limited, very confined way. You may get yourself out of debt, and manage to get by, through holding on or grasping, but that will probably be about it. To experience real wealth, you must let go of holding and grasping, and learn to contain.

We are simultaneously working with two metaphors here, probably more, depending on your ability to contain (ha! ha!). We are working with the metaphor of *you* as the container, as well as a money container being the goal, destination, and form that the energy of money needs to take in order to be made manifest. And in fact the two metaphors are synonymous and co-dependent. If you are unable to contain, you will be unable to create a container, for you are the container!

Hold on to that thought . . .

Everything in life is connected. This is true metaphorically, as well as energetically. This fact can also now be proved through quantum physics. I read somewhere once that sperm cells, even when separated by thousands of miles, maintain a connection for ever. This has been scientifically proven too – quite a thought when choosing a bed mate!

> *I am in you and you in me, mutual in love divine*
> William Blake

So everything is connected, and everything exists by virtue of relationship to everything else. This means that different aspects or areas of life are connected, and also that they affect and reflect one another. How you conduct your personal relationships, for example, will affect and reflect your relationship with money. How you behave in one situation in life pretty much reflects how you will behave in another, seemingly unrelated, context. In fact, one of my own personal maxims is 'How you do anything, is how you do everything'. I absolutely believe this and have observed it to be true throughout my life. Also observably true is that how you do things reflects back to you in how things are done around you.

It is the little things that we are talking about here. It is how we deal with the little, seemingly unimportant things that gives us a real clue into deep underlying patterns that affect our money flow profoundly. It is in the small detail that you can uncover the true nature of something. Those who have worked consciously with people for many years, particularly successful business and sales people, will attest to the fact that one small detail is what it takes to make or break a deal. Always.

The world and people around us are giving us subtle clues and messages all the time, if we would but notice them. If your business relates to people, you train yourself to notice so that you can consciously become aware of what is usually observed only unconsciously.

Let me give you an example. I see my back therapist weekly for half an hour. Yesterday, I mentioned that I might need to bring my son Alex in to my next appointment for a check-up as he'd had a fall. My appointment was set for 1pm and I collect the children from school at 12.30. I mentioned I might be a little late as the children do not always come out of school on time. My therapist has just phoned me to say she has asked her 1.30 appointment to switch with mine so I do not need to feel rushed, in case I do need to bring Alex in. Did she have to do that? No. It is a very little thing, but it means a lot. She does it because she cares. She does it because she runs a very successful practice. And no, it's not the other way round, because it starts off with her doing it, and she was doing this sort of thing before she became successful. She also confirms all her appointments, always – another small but significant detail. She does this because she runs a successful practice. Her name is Irma Stanley-Best (with a name like that, how could you go wrong?).

As you can see, I am focusing on what seem to be small details here, because it is in how we do the things we do not need to that we find the clues as to whether or not we will succeed. I am also saying that everything is linked. If you care about your clients you will care about your staff and your service and the food you prepare, and your business, and you will make money and succeed. It's quite simple, but not always clear.

What has this to do with moneymaking, or being a money container? Well, the knowledge that everything is connected – that all things are in relationship to each other – is one of the cornerstones of my approach. How you do anything is how you do everything. So how you contain money is reflected in other areas of your life. How you contain other aspects of your life is reflected in how you contain money. If you really embrace this concept, you don't need to read the rest of this book! (Well, there is a teeny bit more . . .)

You have already had a look at various aspects of containment in the previous exercises, and you now have your awareness on the metaphor of a container and on the concept on containing things. You are contemplating yourself as container and money as something needing containment. You are also considering the fact that everything is connected, and are putting your awareness to bear on the effect of little actions on wealth creation. This is all a great and wonderful start! An expansion of the way you looked at wealth before. As you expand, so wealth expands because, as I have mentioned, everything is connected. So, you are becoming richer already, even as we speak. Trust me on this!

> *Hold yourself responsible for a higher standard*
> *than anyone else expects of you.*
> *Never excuse yourself.*
> Henry Ward Beecher

It's like trying to catch the wind

Essentially, what we are trying to contain is ourselves. That is what is at the core of all money journeys. Remember schoolteachers saying 'Contain yourself!'? We are containers. We contain our bodies, our emotions, our dreams, our personalities, our talents, our shadow, our various levels of consciousness, our thoughts, our conditioning, our gifts, our secrets, our imaginary friends and selves. We even try to contain our spirit, believing that our bodies contain our spirit when in fact it's the other way round. It is our spirit that contains everything.

Any discussion of a container must begin here, with the realisation that you and I are nothing more than containers – vessels – filled with all manner of things. And how we contain these things, how we contain ourselves, our energy, our beingness, ultimately how we contain our world, and how it contains us is the real issue underpinning any money quest.

How do we contain gossip, bad news, our grievances, our sorrows, our joys? How do we contain our anger, our power, our vision, our energy, our money, our children, our relationships? How do we contain the space around us? These are all different ways of asking the same question. How do we contain? And what does it mean to contain, not just as an act of holding, but as a gesture of accommodation and facilitation? What does it mean to contain as an act of giving, rather than taking? That is the real lesson we have to learn when it comes to money – though this lesson is not confined to money alone, as it also applies to every other area of life.

Finally, the question is how do we contain our love? Or, rather, how do we allow love to contain us and, ultimately, how do we allow our divinity to contain us? But let's not frighten all the business people reading this book away. There *are* business people reading this book, aren't there? You can look at the concept of containment in any depth (really ha! ha!) you like. (Okay, no more ha! ha! I promise!)

Know ye not . . . that the spirit of God dwelleth within you?
I Corinthians 3:16

Light up your life!

It's important to lighten up. None of this is serious. Really. The fact that you can afford to be sitting there reading this book on how to increase your wealth, and the fact that I'm sitting here writing it, puts us both in the top few per cent of truly fortunate people on the planet. So, let's be happy about that!

Back to your wealth container. A container has the following aspects, which we will reflect upon, and work on processing in the following chapters:

I	Shape
II	Material
III	Walls
IV	Base

We have already said that firstly we need a container, and for that to be so we need a SHAPE. One of my ceramics teachers told us once that each person has a signature shape which they produce when they do clay work by hand. I have observed this to be true. In my *Money Well*™ courses, participants create their containers out of clay. This is a symbolic and powerful act which you may want to do for yourself. I will provide details on this later.

Let's look at the shape of your container in the next chapter.

4

The Shape of your Wealth Container

If you don't know the shape, how can you fill it?

Getting into shape

Without shape, you do not have a container, and without a container you cannot contain money. This is what is really meant when we are told to get our finances into shape! So we need to start there, at the end, at the goal, or destination of our journey, because that is where we are going, that is what we want the money for. It's the good old alpha and omega. In the end is the beginning. We need to start at the end. What starting at the end means, in this context, is finding out where you are going, or else you will never get there. Or in other words, know that you have a container and, more specifically, know the definite shape of your container at any one moment in time.

That is one of the secrets of wealth creation. Specificity – a tongue twister of a word! – is also a mind twister. Mind does not like to be pinned down like that. It prefers to wander about, untamed, unconfined, vague. But without specificity, without a defined shape, we have no container, and cannot contain. I am stressing this point because it is important, and because it forms the foundation for the rest of the aspects involved both in the creation of a wealth container and in containing money itself.

For a moment, imagine money as a great flowing river, coming from an endless source (the great Is-ness, or the Reserve Bank, depending on your viewpoint). Imagine money as a formless mass of energy, pure gold, flowing down, drawn inexorably towards the sea, as all rivers are. The river will find its way there. It will fill every dam and lake and waterfall along the way. But no matter what happens, it will continue to move towards the sea.

This is because like is drawn to like, and because the enormous mass of seawater has huge attracting potential, and because the sea is an enormous vacuum to fill and, because nature abhors a vacuum, so therefore the river will fill it. Without the vacuum in fact, there would be no rivers and no water. The water exists to fill the vacuum. Without a container, there will be no money to fill it. Money exists to fill the vacuum or container we create for it. Think of that! Feel that concept with your heart! And, therefore, the more containers we provide, the more money there will be to fill them. Think about that for a moment. Really takes you right away from that 'other' type of thinking, doesn't it?

> *The more containers we create,*
> *the more money there will be to fill them*
> Kiki Theo

You can examine the stories of any successful person from Branson, to Trump, to the café owner down the road (and it's useful to do so), and you will find in all of them the very common, seemingly obvious characteristic of 'a vision'. But we think that vision is synonymous with goal. And because we've heard the word 'goal' thrown about so often; and because we have been harassed by it from childhood; and because some of us have had to sit through endless mind-numbing lectures and meetings on company targets and goals; and because we have had myriad books all titled *Goals, Goals, Goals – and how to 'set' them*; and more recently all manner of coaching and team building, all aimed at ensuring we 'reach' our goals; because of all of this, we've blanked out the word goal from our consciousness, and probably from our unconscious too. We hear it, but we don't.

Kicking the goal

Goal has become one of those clichés like 'be good' and 'eat your greens', and 'coffee is bad for you', and 'stop destroying the ozone layer'. We hear it, but we don't. Start a conversation with someone today about goals and goal setting, and watch their eyes glaze over. Unless they are one of those super achieving Duracell bunnies who are already sold on the idea!

We have heard the word goal so often that it has become denuded of meaning. It may even have acquired anxiety-provoking connotations becoming, rather than a source of inspiration, another item on the (as yet) unaccomplished 'to do' list, together with those New Year resolutions: 1. Dark chocolate covered roasted almonds – STOP EATING! 2. Get regular exercise. 3. Set realistic goals for this year, and so on.

> *Is not life a thousand times too short for us to bore ourselves?*
> Friedrich Nietzsche

The clichéd goal and goal setting that most of us are allergic to, is goal 'set' in terms of measurement, achievement, winning, aspiring, and being driven. We think it has to do with aiming for something solid out there and moving towards getting it, often with the added dimension of a time limit, accompanied by reams of lists, budgets, business plans and affirmations, while chased by Competing Others also after our 'precious'. Very serious stuff. Very grown-up. Not much fun. And so if we so much as hear the word 'goal' whispered we blank it out, straight away – and who could blame us?

29

I'm too sexy for my cat

I don't know about you, but when it comes down to it, I just wanna have fun! Really. In fact I had a profound revelation one night, about a quarter of century ago now (you can say that when you're almost fifty!). A friend and I went to see the band Right Said Fred live in a club in Johannesburg as we both love dancing. Remember that totally nonsensical song 'I'm too sexy for my shirt/cat/hat?' Well, I really loved the fact that someone was not taking life or themselves too seriously, so off we went.

It was such absolute, over the top, *FUN!* We laughed and laughed and danced and danced. I came home and wrote a piece about my realisation that we are here to learn how to party – to lighten up and have fun. *'One day, when we get to heaven',* I wrote, *'I think God will be asking us, "Have you learnt to party?" and regardless of anything else, if we haven't learnt to lighten up and have fun . . . well, it'll be back into the litter tray!'* I still believe this. (Whatever happened to Right Said Fred? They used to wear those really fun pants with the back pockets cut out . . .)

Anyhow, Serious Goal 'Setting' (like some sort of cutting into stone) is definitely out! In order to take our wealth to the next level, we need to update our thinking about Goal, redefine and refine it. We need to perceive Goal differently. We need to shift our perspective to Goal as a destination; as a state of beingness we are trying to achieve; as a feeling we would like to experience; and as a container for the energy of money to flow into. Ultimately we need to see our container as that which will draw and accommodate our wealth, like the sea attracts the river.

What sort of cat?

And to do that means we must get specific. Our wealth container needs *shape*. What will that shape be? The shape of our container sets up the path of attainment of our goal. The shape of our container invokes our will and our intent. The shape of our container denotes commitment. We need to ask to receive – that means we know what we are asking for. The shape of our container shows us what it is not – a saucer is not a cup. Most of all, the shape of our container is a feeling and a new beingness we want to achieve. And we need to own that. To contain means to own. And that is a wonderful pun indeed. In fact it is also a truism. (Perhaps the correct word is puntrism . . . Should I trademark that, I wonder?) When you set your heart on something, you give your container shape. When you decide that **THIS** is what I want, not that, or that, but **THIS**, then you have the makings of a container. When you decide to give up compromising, and making do, and settling for, and that horror of horrors called 'doing my best' (I mean what sort of sorry cop-out is *that*?), then you have the makings of a container.

Decide what it is that you truly, truly, want. Don't be afraid to say it. No matter how naff or silly, or impractical or meaningful or meaningless you think others may think it is. It's none of their business anyway. Infuse your container with all the joy or the security or the power that you want your wealth to bring. Find out what it is you want your wealth to make you feel. And feel it! Then, focus all of your efforts and attention not on *how* the container will be filled, but rather on how to make it strong and durable and large enough and beautiful enough to attract and to contain pure gold – the gold of your soul.

If I keep a green bough in my heart, the singing bird will come
Chinese Proverb

In other words, stop worrying about *how* you will get the money and start thinking of *what* you will do with it, and how you will feel when you get it.

The basic difference between people who achieve tremendous things and those who don't, is that the achievers are totally focused on *what* they are creating, whereas the others spend all their time and energy worrying about *how* to get what they want (when they may not even know what that is). When you get down to asking people what they would do if they had all the money in the world, most of them simply don't know.

What will you *do* with the money? Or in other words, imagine you are face to face with the money genii, or the wish-fulfilling fairy, or a potential investor (depending on your sense of humour).

They have the means and the desire to give you as much money as you want – no limit – you need fulfil only two conditions.

- Number One: you need to be totally honest (they have trutho-meters, or in the case of the investor, accountants ready to inflict due diligence), and
- Number Two: you need to be pretty specific about what you want.

Are you ready to fulfil these simple conditions? Are you? Of course there is also a third, probably most important, most obvious, yet often most overlooked requirement, and that is *asking*.

We are told to ask, seek, knock, before we can receive, find, or have the door opened. Are you ready for that too?

Ask and you will receive . . .

What does all that mean in the 'real' world? It's all very well in our metaphorical, symbolic world, and certainly it is easy and neces-sary to start there, but what do we do 'out there'? What all these words – ask, seek, knock – have in common is action. And before action comes a choice, a decision, a focus, an intent, and these too are all active. And all of this action is never possible without a commitment. But first you need a decision, and a choice. That decision, that commitment – to approach the wish-fulfilling fairy, the investor, the well of gold, the river of money – that decision and commitment to expand your wealth, in every sense of the word, and to open up the potential of a new you, *that* is the start.

To ask means to be ready to receive. To be ready to receive means you

1. know what you are asking for, and
2. can accommodate or *contain* it when you receive it.

It takes time to become ready to receive. In the case of a baby it takes nine months from conception; in the case of a new house a few months for transfer, or many months or years to build from scratch; in the case of enlightenment, many lifetimes, we are told.

If you do not know what you are asking for you will never get it. This is obvious. So asking is synonymous with knowing in this context. Knowing what you want. Making a choice. Saying '*This is what I want*'.

This requires great courage in a world that either tells us we should want all sorts of things that we may not, or condemns us for wanting to pursue other things. The courage to stand up for what we want, and to go even further than that to committing to pursue and get what we want, requires a high level of honesty, a high degree of self-knowledge, and a commitment to follow our own personal truth.

Ask, ask, and ask again

So asking is a profound and powerful act. As is seeking and knocking. It is profound and powerful because to acknowledge and to stand up for our truth is the most important thing we can do.

I remember meeting an attorney in the late seventies. His father had been an attorney, as had his before him. So this young man had been raised with the expectation that he follow in the footsteps of his forefathers. He had studied and become a lawyer. And he hated it.

Now this is the story of many a boy or girl, and it usually ends with the lawyer, or the accountant, or the seamstress or the baker settling for the money, and the security, and doing the 'logical' thing (after all the years of study, and the cost, and the parents' sacrifices), and living (not quite) happily ever after.

But this young lawyer did not. And, yes, he was newly married and the couple were expecting a baby, so he had the sort of responsibilities we are taught to honour above the pursuit of our truth. But this young man, let's call him Sam, gave up his practice and guess what he did? He got a job as the manager of a large furniture store! This is absolutely a true story. And he told me he was loving it!

Now there are very few people who would not regard a job as a furniture store manager as less prestigious, lucrative, important, meaningful or desirable than being a lawyer. And Sam probably had to stare into their incredulous faces every day. But he did it anyway. Well done, Sam! We salute you!

Don Juan says in one of Carlos Castaneda's books that if only we gave up our sense of self-importance, not only would we have an enormous amount of energy available (which is what it takes to maintain self-importance), but we would also be able to truly see the splendour of the world around us.

We don't all want to build magnificent towers or save the world. Most of us just want to live ordinary, simple, but abundant lives. Most of us just want to be happy.

I want to drive a Cadillac

It took an enormous amount of courage for Sam to turn his back on law and, indirectly, on his forefathers and pursue a seemingly menial position as a furniture store manager. It takes enormous courage to say to your success-driven family, 'I want to go and save the seahorses'; 'No thanks, I really don't want to be an accountant'; 'So sorry, I don't want to take over the multimillion-dollar family businesses'; 'No, really, I don't want that luxury house on the beach, I want to live in an eco village in a cob house'. It takes a lot of truth and courage and balls to do that (even if you are a girl – girls have balls).

It takes as much courage to do that as it does to tell your spiritually orientated, green, socially conscious family that you want to create an empire. 'No, Mom, I don't want to live in an ecological cob house, I want a luxury condo.' 'Yes, Dad, I know about the ozone layer, but I really *love* this convertible.' 'I know it's God's temple, Mum, but I'm having the implants.' All this takes courage too.

The courage to speak your truth. And once you find what that truth is, and are willing to stand by it (of course it is part of the Divine's cosmic joke that you will be placed in a position or in a family to have this truth if not discredited, at least severely questioned – that's just the way things are), then you have taken the first step. Then you are ready to *ask*. Well, almost ready.

Because linked to asking is the readiness to receive or, in other words, having a container, which is the subject of this book. Funny how everything is linked, isn't it?

In a brief recap: we were seated with our money genii or wish-fulfilling fairy or investor (often this is the very same person in disguise) and they were willing and able to grant us any amount of money, provided we were honest and specific about what we wanted. We dealt with *asking* as the key element in this exchange, and determined that asking is linked to, if not synonymous with, knowing what we want, which in turn fulfils both the conditions of honesty and specificity. We have said that it all starts with making a commitment to honouring your truth. When you do that, you are almost ready to ask, because an integral part of asking is the readiness to receive.

And all of *that* has to do with determining the *shape* of your container, which is also your destination, and it is also your new beingness. So, back to being ready, or becoming ready to receive.

Becoming ready to receive has to do with faith and trust, going out on a limb, miracles and wonders, signs, signals and omens, crazy illogical acts, or just sheer optimism. Certainly, it's another act, it's something you have to do. You cannot do nothing. This is important.

Leaving the door of possibility open, or 'Yet' . . .

Being ready to receive means leaving the possibility of receiving open. It is holding the space ready for the manifestation to take place (more on this in my book *The Art of Conscious Creation*. What? You thought you were going to skip the ads?). To put it differently, let me tell you a true story:

Once upon a time in deepest, darkest Africa (in one of the cities), there lived a man of modest means. He worked hard every day and then went home to his modest house where his faithful wife was waiting with a home-cooked meal. Their children went to school, and although all their needs were met through careful saving and budgeting, there was never anything left over for really special treats or holidays. Moreover, the man had a dream, a very large dream. He wanted to own a big beautiful house for his family and he also wished he could provide one for his parents and one for his married sister too.

Every week he faithfully bought a lotto ticket. Every week, he he would drive around the suburb he had selected for the family homes, and he would imagine the whole of his family living side by side in the three beautiful houses he had selected.

And, yes, of course he won! He'd already picked the houses, you see.

Being ready to receive is akin to making the commitment with no turning back. It's giving up your day job and becoming a full-time musician. It's leaving no room for failure, burning your bridges, going for it. Being ready to receive is the Bible story of preparing the great feast in anticipation of the groom arriving. Those who did not prepare did not receive him.

Being ready to receive is me, sitting here writing this, my *second* book, as a full-time 'occupation' having taken a sabbatical from delivering both money courses and business coaching to focus on writing, some six months ago. I sit here practising to be a fully fledged 'writer' when, to date, I have received something like nine rejections for the publication of my first book from various agents and publishers abroad.[1] I sit here gamely telling you about my *next* book, book number three, *The Art of Conscious Creation*, when my first book is still not published. Yet. As things stand right now, you have not even read my first book. Yet. And it is the Yet which is the place of being ready to receive. It is the Yet which is the doorway into the future me – the published, best-selling author. It is the Yet which is that tentative ephemeral space of containing the dream.

But do you know that as I sit here writing, in my make-believe occupation as a make-believe author, to my make-believe audience, with input from time to time from my make-believe editor, having to stop in between for some make-believe signings of books and promotions around the world, do you know that *you* are sitting there also waiting for my book?

And do you know that as I sit here writing, there is *no doubt* in my mind that you will want to, and need to, and *expect* to read this book after you have read the first one! And I also absolutely know you will *love* the first one, which of course you will have read by the time you read this. (If you haven't read *Money Alchemy* yet, please

---

[1] I wrote those words in June 2007. Since then I have revised the draft of *The Money Well* a few times. More importantly, since writing those words, *Money Alchemy* has been published by Penguin as part of a two book deal!

go and get a copy, already!) All of this belief fits into that little space of Yet. So I write this for you. And as you are definitely real as you sit there reading this book, so then all this is real too.

And that, ladies and gentlemen, *that* is 'being ready to receive'. Definitely not something you can explain to Mum. Elvis has left the building.

> *Your own words are the bricks and mortar of the dreams you*
> *want to realise.*
> *The words you choose and use, establish the life you experience*
> Sonia Choquette

Are you ready to receive? Let's do some processing on that.

If you are not able to do the processing now, skip to the next section, and come back to this later. But do come back! The successful transformation of your wealth container depends on doing *the processing!*

In the following exercise you will uncover and observe habitual sayings and transform them into words of power which you will adopt as new wealth beliefs. You will also create a wish list, infuse it with emotion, and execute inspired action that will help you to prepare to receive the items on your list.

> *Before you start, STATE YOUR INTENT! Be clear and specific. For example:*
> *'It is my intent that this processing will release the flow of wealth in my life and I am able to contain it.'*
> *Keep your pen moving*
> *Write without thinking*
> *Repeat the prompt if you are stuck*
> *Keep it light!*

Part One: Say it Again with Oomph!
Wealth Training Process

In this section we will focus our attention on the way we phrase things in everyday life, with the intention of creating words of power that will support and energise our wealth vision.

- Write a list of ten 'vague', non-specific expressions you use when you ask (or wish, or lust, or hope, or dream) for money to come your way. For example, 'I want *enough* for me and my family', or 'I want to be *comfortable*', or even 'I want to be *extremely wealthy*', or 'I want to have *lots of money*'.

- Ask close family and friends to tell you what they hear you saying too – this can be quite a revelation.
- Working *lightly,* with reflection, and with the intent of becoming crystal clear in what you want, rephrase each expression into something specific, clear, and real. Let your heart speak. Ensure your beliefs do not contain anything negative – for example, change 'I want no debt' to 'I want all my accounts in credit'. This is a very important step, do not omit it.
- Practise saying the new expressions out loud. Use them in your daily speech.
- Adopt your new sayings as new beliefs.

It is good to do this practice regularly. Slowly, you will peel away layers of surface blah blah to reveal your true innermost wants and needs. This will clarify the shape of your container. It will also firm and solidify its texture – which will be our next point of reflection. Most importantly, it will add power to your words.

Part Two: Preparing to Receive
Wealth Training Process

1. List the top ten *specific* things you want right now in your life (no vagueness, adjectives, or ego).
   For example: 1. I want a new wardrobe of clothes
   2. I want a classical guitar
   3. I want a credit balance in my cheque account
2. Add to each one the feeling you are after with each want (yes to adjectives, still no to the rest).
   For example: next to 1 above, could be: 'slim, happy and sexy'
   next to 2 above could be: 'creative, fun, light'
   next to 3 above could be : 'wealthy, free, powerful'
3. Rate each one and pick the three most important, zingiest ones (those that make your heart zing, not your mind. They do not need to be 'logical' or 'feasible').

4. Now, list five things you need to do in respect of each item to become ready to receive. These are actual, physical things to do – *not* cop-outs like 'believing more' or 'having faith' or 'trusting', or '*trying* this or that'. Ask yourself 'What do I need *to do* to be ready to receive this thing that I want?' Symbolic acts are acceptable as *one, only one,* of the five items. For example, for 'a new wardrobe of clothes' could be:

    (a)   Pick out of wardrobe all the clothes that don't fit, or don't make me feel slim, sexy, or happy

    (b)   Give away some to charity; sell some; swap some with a friend

    (c)   Adjust, repair, and remodel any clothes I like into new creations

    (d)   Go out and try on clothes that fit, that I want, that make me feel 'slim, sexy, and happy'

5. Perform the acts with the right feeling, attention, and intent.

6. Ask yourself again, 'What do I need to do, to be ready to receive this thing that I want?'

7. Perform the acts with the right feeling, attention, and intention.

8. Continue with steps 6 and 7 until you are ready to receive. This may take longer than a day but, let's face it, so did the creation of the world, so do not become discouraged. Meanwhile, while the cauldron is brewing, continue with the book.

9. Be ready to receive! Expect the most wonderful things to happen! Celebrate and rejoice! Remember to consciously acknowledge and give thanks for what is received too!

Being ready to receive is linked to asking. And as asking is linked to knowing what we want, it is often that *knowing* which is the preparation we require. We need to become more specific about what we want. If you are unclear about what you want, you will be unable to prepare to receive. Without knowing what you want, you cannot create the shape of your container. And without a container you cannot create or maintain wealth.

Don't forget 'the obvious'

Simplicity is an art form. Developing clarity of mind is a lifelong practice. We live in such a complex world that often the most obvious, simple facts elude us. Often, when I work with companies, for example, I find that the most simple fact – such as, the purpose of a company is firstly to make a profit – becomes lost in a sea of well-meaning intentions and company procedures. Yes, of course people come first, and it's great to have wonderful company policy that enables share ownership for staff, and naturally you need to deliver a great product, BUT unless you are clear on the fact that any company's purpose must be to make a profit, your company may simply never survive long enough for you to do any of those other things. You need to be clear on your intent.

The purpose of a sales person in a company, for example, is to produce – to make sales, to achieve targets, better still to exceed targets. Yes, of course they should be honest and loyal and so on, but if they do not deliver sales as a primary prerequisite, all those other things will not help. Get clear. Get specific. Train yourself to see the obvious – first. Be clear.

Know what you want, be specific, and don't forget the obvious. Now let's look at another aspect of the shape of your container, its interest or fun value.

Back to fun, I like that!

Who can contain the flow of the river?

Imagine that untold wealth is rushing towards you, even as we speak. It is powerful, ancient, massive, formless energy, looking for a home, yearning to take form. It flows towards you gathering momentum like an avalanche, like a torrent, like a river in flood. How will you contain this force? Where will you house it? How will you tame it, charm it to be with you? What will you offer it to attract its attention?

Here's Donald offering to transform money into a holiday island filled with hotels and a magnificent theme park – lots of bling and babes and fun cocktails with little pink umbrellas. There's Richard tempting it to become a fleet of spaceships that will fly people to the moon – power, excitement, frontier breaking stuff. And you want to change it to a positive balance on your credit card? Come on, you can do better than that!

Why should money come to you?

That question deserves its own paragraph. I have heard many strange reasons for people wanting, and in some cases demanding, that money comes to them, though I'm sure money has heard far stranger ones than I have. There was, for example, an organisation which, although it had the best of intentions, said that the reason a certain very wealthy individual should fund their project was simply because the person 'had so much money they would not miss it'. This was the basis of their thinking and of their vision.

You've gotta be kidding!

If you come to the well of plenty with a bucket full of holes, you will not be able to fill your container. And, indeed, you may need to address the holes in your argument when you declare that money needs to come to you. You do not have a claim over your neighbour's bounty because you think he has too much and will not miss it. You cannot demand the lady with the big full container should give you some of hers even though you don't even have a container yourself, or yours is tiny and leaks. We will deal with leaks and blocks later and at length in Part II of this book – 'Transforming Leaks and Blocks to Wealth Flow'.

WHY SHOULD MONEY COME TO YOU? Let's face it, money is pretty much in demand. Mr Moola is getting invitations all over the place, all the time, 24/7 as they say. You can imagine him reclining in his silk smoking jacket and cravat in the drawing room of his country estate. Very Merchant Ivory. Rupert Everett would do well in the role.

The butler arrives with a silver tray piled high with invitations.

'More invitations, sir,' he says.

'Thank you, Reeves. Anything interesting?'

'Not really, sir. Usual stuff. Debt, car repayments, alimony, better house . . . Oh yes, there was something I think . . . let me see . . . Here. Yes, this may interest you, sir. It's this chap Richard again, sir. He plans to do trips to the moon . . .'

'Trips to the moon, hey? Now *that* sounds like fun! Pack my bags, Reeves, I think we'll respond to that one.'

Reality cheque, please

One of the participants on my *Money Alchemy* course wrote in her course feedback, 'I have had a complete shift – money moves like energy – is attracted to the extraordinary, fun and colourful – it is easy to access with the right mindset.' And that is exactly it, except that I would add 'and feeling' to the end of the sentence, as that is an absolutely necessary ingredient.

Why would money be attracted to the extraordinary, the fun and the colourful? For the same reason we are. And, after all, let us not become confused with the use of these metaphors and fabulous illustrations – at the end of the day we are talking about **US**. **WE** are the energy, the money, the container, the goal, the destination, the new beingness . . . and so on. **WE** are the creators of this whole reality.

> *Those who lose dreaming are lost*
> Australian Aboriginal proverb

So why would money be attracted by the Fun and Colourful? For the same reason we would be! Because it's Fun and Colourful! Fun and Colourful is more interesting than drab and dull – ask any toddler. Fun and Colourful is more attractive, it draws us more. Fun and Colourful has more energy, and we need energy for the creation of anything. Remember how a rocket uses 90 per cent of its fuel for take-off, and how this is also true for any venture, dream, goal we may have? We need energy. Fun and Colourful has more.

Last, but most importantly, Fun and Colourful (and Extraordinary and Magical) make us *feel good* and it is this feel good factor that will attract all good things to us, especially money. Because without a feel good feeling, nothing will happen. We will discuss this further in the next section.

So what we have is not only that we must know what we want clearly enough to be able to ask for it, but that this thing we want must be fun and colourful enough to attract us (and money) through creating a good feeling. Is that not a bit of a tall order, if not downright unreal and childish? I mean most people just want an ordinary life, a good home and car, and to put the kids through school comfortably, nothing extraordinary, just ordinary survival. And if that's what you want that's fine, because survival is what you will get, nothing wrong with that. But why can't 'basic survival' become an art form? Why can it not be graceful and fun and effortless and rewarding?

And that, you cannot get without being clear about it and feeling good – not unless you want to put your health and well-being at risk. Furthermore, it would seem that mere survival is simply not good enough for us, the more conscious of the species. It would seem that beyond survival we want, perhaps even need, transcendence. And this desire to become more takes many forms – everything from climbing Mount Everest, to setting new records, to becoming enlightened. We have an inbuilt need to become more, or to move beyond basic survival. We see this everywhere. Nature is forever abundant and creative.

So in fact it is neither unrealistic nor impractical to say to you: When you know what you want clearly enough to be able to ask for it, and when that thing that you ask for is so connected with your innermost wants and needs and truth that it makes your heart sing, and when you feel so good about that thing, that you are ready to receive it, because you feel the way you would feel when you do receive it, *then* you have created the shape of your wealth container, and automatically set up the flow of wealth, and that thing's attainment, towards you.

> *Without this playing with fantasy,*
> *no creative work has ever come to birth*
>
> Carl G Jung

A little note on symbol

Carl Jung placed great value on the use of symbol, not only as a means of accessing information locked in the unconscious, but also as a way to release large amounts of energy. Working with metaphor, as we are doing here, is a way of working with symbol. When we work with symbol we enter the land of infinite possibility, the land of imagination and dreams. It is a land where anything is possible, and where everything can be transformed. For that is

43

the ultimate purpose of symbol – transformation.

We use metaphor, image, symbol, as a means of engaging that part of ourselves which is the alchemist, the wizard, the creator of magic in our lives. Symbol is a very personal thing. Its message is only for you to understand – you who give it its meaning. Symbol is sacred, mystical, powerful. Sometimes a symbol simply conveys an emotion – there need be no logic to the use of symbol.

- When working with symbol, be it in 'drawing' your container, engaging in writing about money as metaphor, or creating your container out of clay, it is important to be aware that you are working with symbol. Allow the symbol to speak to you in whichever way it does. Do not judge or analyse too much.
- Do not strip away the energy or feeling that the symbol evokes for you in favour of smart analysis.
- If you (really) need to, receive input, not judgement, from a very trusted friend or teacher only.
- It is good to put your drawing or clay work where you can see it daily, so you can absorb its essence. When you become bored with looking at it, its work is done, and you can put it away.

Wrapping it all up

To contain money you need a container. The most basic element of a container is its shape. The shape of a container must remain constant at any moment in time in order to be able to contain. The shape of your container is your specific goal or destination. Your goal or destination is also a feeling that you want to feel. It is a new you with a new beingness. To connect with this new destination, or wealth vision, you need to ask or seek within your heart. Once you know what you want, how that feels, and are willing to commit to getting it, you are ready to *ask*, and to prepare to receive. Being ready to receive is holding a space for your dream to unfold. It requires faith and optimism, and holding on to that feeling.

When you know exactly what you want, are committed enough to getting it to ask, and are confident enough to expect to receive it, then you have created the shape of your container, which is the beginning of wealth's journey towards you. (Yes, verily, Mr Moola is packing his trunk even as we speak – well, Reeves is packing anyway.)

5

The Material of Your Wealth Container

Can your dream withstand the weather?

Sugar and spice and all that's nice . . .

Is that what your container is made of? I do hope so. The texture of your container must be firm yet expandable. The material your container is made of must be strong enough to weather storms, yet supple enough to stretch itself to new limits. You want a container that is sturdy and dependable. You want a container you can rely on. Are you like that? I do hope so. You want a container that will get the job done, that will hold its contents and not spill them. You want a container that will contain!

What your container is made of is akin to its skin. We are looking at the surface of something and how that affects what is below.

It's a little like what we were saying earlier about looking at and changing the way we express desire for wealth. Because it is not only the unconscious that affects the conscious, it is also the other way around. Because as above, so below and as below, so above. And also because everything is connected!

So what you do on the 'outside' will affect the inside. Beauty is not really skin deep . . . This means that if you are not clear about what you want, if your boundaries and parameters (or walls) are not clear, if your boundaries with yourself and the rest of the world are not clear, then the material that makes up your container will not be optimum. It means your walls may be shaky and it may even mean that the shape of your container will be unclear and therefore your container will remain unformed. This will mean, in effect, that you do not have a container, and without one, you cannot contain wealth.

Strong, durable, supple material – that is what is needed. And, as we have already said that we are the container, and we are the destination, the question becomes: Are you cultivating the qualities of strength, durability and suppleness in yourself, and are you bringing these qualities to your wealth journey?

> *Our skin is what stands between us and the world*
> Diane Ackerman

Let's look at the strength of your container. Strength speaks of strength of will. Cultivating the will is key to developing strength of purpose, strength of intent, and staying power. We generally see the word 'will' as something rather negative, as in wilful children, pets or lovers, we see it as a form of stubbornness, or petulance, or intractability. We are coaxed and forced and in the old days were beaten out of our will as children and teenagers. And later as adults on the spiritual path we try to surrender our will to Higher Powers. However, you need to have the will before you can surrender it. Many people do not succeed on their wealth journey simply because they lack the proper use of will. And this is because they have never properly trained their will in the first place.

Where there's a will there's a way

Yes, I am on a mission to use up every single cliché ever created in this book! However, these old proverbs have withstood the test of time because they are Verily True! And there is not one of you reading this book who can tell me that you have never been in a position in your life when you tested and proved this particular proverb to be true!

So, how do you cultivate the will? By using it, by stretching yourself, by keeping your word, through practice. Will and wuss do not go together. Will and willy-nilly, namby-pamby do not go together. Will and ego do not go together. Will and pandering to neuroses do not go together. Will and excuses do not go together. Will and preciousness do not go together.

Will is about getting out of your excuses and smallness of thinking and judgement and special-ness and focusing and *DOING* it, *NOW* ALREADY! Cultivating the will is a form of practice greatly enhanced by meditation – where meditation is sitting with what is, being in the present, observing thoughts and emotions arising, not relaxation to the sound of calming music while you drift off to other lands.

Will and Word are almost synonymous. The power of the word is only such because of the will behind the word. And vice versa. If you can keep your word in little things, you will keep your word in bigger things. And vice versa. Because, yes, everything is connected. You can really save yourself an incredible amount of time, energy and money in business, and in your wealth quest if you embrace this concept.

> *Your words are the greatest power you have*
> Sonia Choquette

Do it from the heart

The way you do anything IS the way you do everything. If you can rely on someone to do what they say they will do in small matters, then you can absolutely rely on them to keep their word in bigger matters. And vice versa. How you do what you don't really *need* to do is how you will do things at the end of the day. That's actually a more accurate way of putting things. How reliable are you? How well do you keep your word? How dependable are you? Because that is exactly how reliable and dependable your container will be.

Now, the good news is that putting attention and intention on these aspects of ourselves enables us to make some profound changes, quite quickly. And remember, what we are doing here is strengthening the material our container is made of, so that it becomes more durable. Also remember that, as everything is connected, a change performed in one area of our lives will affect other areas, especially if done with specific and focused intent.

Returning to will for a moment, I would like to refer to Reshad Feild, from his book *Alchemy of the Heart*. He has a whole chapter entitled 'Will', which I suggest you read. Feild says that we cannot fulfil the will of God without will, and nor can God's will be fulfilled without us.

We need both the will and the willingness to do it. We cannot surrender our will to God if we have no will in the first place!

Will implies responsibility, Feild goes on to say. We need to be conscious and we need to be completely in the moment, in the present, able to respond to what is needed, which is what responsibility is really all about.

Feild concludes with some advice on how will can be developed. He suggests that after a really clear intent to develop will has been established, we put in a little bit of extra effort into everything we do – try to do everything at ten per cent more than usual.

This is the concept of *arista*, or excellence, that Greeks aspire towards. It is the notion that when we are finished, or nearly finished, or even when we feel quite finished, we can put in just a little more energy. This is pushing beyond the limits, this is raising our ceiling into 'the beyond' which is the land where anything is possible.

Making decisions is another way of cultivating will. By making decisions and then executing the decisions we have made, we strengthen our will considerably. In this way, writes Feild, we not only 'overcome the forces of hazard' and avoid being 'tossed by the hands of fate', but we are also 'given help from higher worlds', making it possible for God's grace to enter.

We are talking about a container for our wealth. And we are looking at the material the container is made of as being durable, supple, flexible and dependable. We are looking at how these qualities are expressions of our own dependability, capacity to deliver, ability to keep our word, and at how these qualities are all expressions of the proper use of will. We have now looked at cultivating the will through intention, completing the tasks we set ourselves, putting extra effort into the things we do, and making decisions.

Phew! Who would have thought that talking about something as simple as a container could raise so much to think about, discuss and absorb? Time for a breather. Take a tea or coffee break now!

> *You must push yourself beyond your limits, all the time*
> Carlos Castaneda from *Don Juan*

In the following process you will create a container and observe it as part of your reflection practice. You will also firm up your will and add power to your voice and the material of your container by executing some inspired action. You will reflect on your own skin as metaphor for the material of your wealth container while bathing – getting the wealth under your skin, so to speak. Finally, you will create a new container and observe how your authentic action and skin reflection have altered the appearance of this container compared to the first one you wrote about earlier in the book.

If you are not able to do the processing now, skip to the next section, and come back to this later. But do come back! The successful transformation of your wealth container depends on doing *the processing! And it's a real fun process!*

Creating more durable material for your container

If the skin of your container needs a facelift (and, let's face it, who could not use one of those?), you may want to consider the following:

Before you start, STATE YOUR INTENT! Be clear and specific. For example:
> *'It is my intent that this processing will release the flow of wealth in my life and I am able to contain it.'*

Keep your pen moving
Mould and create/Write without thinking
Repeat the prompt if you are stuck
Keep it light!

A. Creating the Container – or seeing what's there
Wealth Training Process

1. Find a quiet space. Using a ball of clay, play dough, or dough made from flour and water, the size of your palm, work the clay till it feels ready and then create a small container.
2. Put your intention on improving the material of your container and observe the texture, thickness, flexibility and other qualities that may come to mind.
3. Keep it light – both the exercise and the clay.
4. Make any changes needed to the clay with intention, that is, add water, more flour or clay, make the walls of the container thinner or thicker, until you are satisfied.
5. Set your container aside where you can see it daily. Simply observe.

B. Changing your Skin, on one ... two ... three
Wealth Training Process

1. Do this a few days after creating your container. Complete each item, that is, the listing *and* doing, before going on to the next item. Just listing will not do. State your intent before you start. Your intent here is to clarify and enhance the material of your wealth container. Lightly, with joy!
2. List three decisions you need to make which you have been delaying. Take the decisions. Act. (This can be something as simple as deciding what colour to paint the hallway, or as complicated as deciding which staff member to promote and which to transfer.)

3. List three things you need to deliver on. Deliver. (This can be anything from returning that book you said you would last week, to making that call that may help an acquaintance get a job.)
4. List three incomplete cycles in your life. Complete them. (We will be dealing with cycles and their completion at length in Part II – Transforming Leaks and Blocks to Wealth Flow.) An incomplete cycle is something you have started but not finished. For example, 'Finish filing away my papers'.
5. List three occasions when you did not keep your word. Rectify the situation. (Perhaps you have been promising to watch one of your son's cricket matches, or to write a letter to the paper about noise pollution.)
6. Do three things at 10 per cent above your usual limit. (Yes, even sex could count, why not? And if not sex, what about finding a new topic of conversation at a silent or negative dinner table?)

I am what is around me
Wallace Stevens

C. Sensing the Skin beneath your Skin
Wealth Training Process

1. Have a long, deep soak in a bath with bubbles and scents and candles – even if you're a man.
2. Examine and reflect upon your skin and its qualities. Keep this reflection light and frothy.
3. Marvel on how the skin contains all your organs and every part of your body. How it can shrink or expand, how it breathes, how it is waterproof, yet can absorb water, how it can hear (according to Dr Alfred Tomatis skin is undifferentiated ear), how it can sense, how it protects us from pollutants and disease, how it is a barrier between us and the world. Reflect on all of this and whatever else comes up for you.
4. Ask your skin what it needs from you at this time to enhance itself. Do what is required. (Does it want you to use a loofah, or perhaps a massaging oil?)
5. Note your reflections and observations as well as any decisions taken or acts needed in your Money Book once you're dry. (That's

the book you have been doing all your writing in all this time – refer to instructions at the end of the book, page 250.)

D. Putting it all Together, or Do it Again, Samantha
Wealth Training Process

1. Allow a few days to pass before doing the final section of this processing, while neutrally observing and noting anything that arises in your day-to-day life.
2. Repeat the whole of 'Section A – Creating the Container' – above.
3. Compare, without judgement, any changes between the first and second container. (Write about this if you would like to.)
4. Be amazed! Be joyful! Be ready to receive! Be ready to go to the next section!
5. Remember to acknowledge and give thanks for your wins.

Do it any which way you can!

By now you are probably getting a very clear idea that there are very many ways in which you can make significant and positive changes to your wealth profile without having to resort to the traditional methods (like work, or budgets, or bankers . . . !). You can repeat any of this processing; in fact I recommend that you do, from time to time. It will continue to yield results.

We have looked at the material a container is made of as being akin to skin in terms of flexibility and being a barrier. We have linked it to dependability, and keeping one's word and we have also looked at will as an important component of this. The last aspect of what makes up the material of a container that we will be looking at, is probably the most important of all, certainly in terms of the creation process, and that is emotion, as this is the glue that will hold everything together.

Can you feel it?

The shape of your container or your destination/goal must evoke the feeling you want to feel once your container is full. In other words, you need to connect to what it will feel like once you have arrived at this new destination. And hopefully that is a good feeling

Emotion, in particular feeling good, is the beacon that will attract the river of money to you. It is also the glue that holds the material of your container together. Without emotion, strong emotion, visualising what you want, even if it's in Technicolor, will not guarantee results. This is a key component in the creation process, so I will be spending some time on it.

There has been much talked and written about positive thinking which is usually linked to affirmations, and focusing only on the good, which can become a real challenge if you're not part of the always-look-on-the-bright-side brigade.

Positive thinking has become a little like the goal setting I mentioned earlier. Something we gloss over, agree with, but don't hear any more, and not what I am talking about when I speak about evoking a good feeling.

The thing about 'positive' thinking is that its mere existence implies that there is also this other 'negative' thinking that is not as good. However, thinking is thinking. Thoughts arise in the mind. None are particularly positive or negative, they are just thoughts. How we engage with them, interpret them and so on is what makes us experience them as good or bad, positive or negative. Left to their own devices (which is a skill we try to develop in meditation), thoughts will simply drift by, without our having to have any involvement with them whatsoever.

Don't take your thoughts for a drive

A learned lama once gave the example of standing on the side of the road watching taxis drive past. The taxis are like our thoughts – we can just watch them go by. We do not have to stop a taxi and get in, and go for a drive, and then discover it is not a very nice car, it has no air conditioning or sunroof, so I don't like it, so I am now unhappy; I think I will try this other taxi, oh this is much better, it has a CD player but, oh no, I don't like this music very much . . . You can see where this goes.

Thoughts are thoughts. And yes, it is of course better, if we are to entertain any of them at all, that we choose those thoughts that uplift and motivate and give us energy. Here, however, we are talking about the feel-good factor that must infuse the material of our container, if we are truly to realise our goals. And I am saying that this is not the same as affirmation-induced positive thinking which is generally aimed at reconditioning or reprogramming the unconscious.

Step into that feeling

Feeling good – which also means generating a certain energy which is irresistible, which also means being open to receiving, which also means feeling uplifted, which also means being centred, which means being the co-creator of that which is created, which means expecting to receive all good things, which means being in the present and being connected to the core of your creative soul, which in a nutshell means raising your vibration – is what I am talking about.

This is a space and a frequency that you can learn to tune into. It takes practice. You need to learn how to locate it within your body, how to move it around. I will briefly describe the process later. There is also a whole book written on this subject alone, *Excuse me, your life is waiting* by Lynn Grabhorn, which is well worth reading. (See Bibliography for details.)

All great sales people, public speakers, motivational teachers, actors, in fact all performers, have learnt how to enter a feel-good space at will. It is simply a part of the job. The difference between the good and the great performers is that the good ones imitate a good feel face, whereas the great ones tune into the frequency. You can tell the difference in the eyes. No one wakes up feeling great *every, single* day!

On occasion I have had to face the start of a course with a migraine, and once with food poisoning and, let's face it, who wants to be taught or instructed by someone in pain? But thanks to all the years of working with people in service, I have learnt how to enter into a feel-good space at will, no matter how my body is feeling. And it's not faking at all, because people can tell when you are faking. In fact, faking is something you can tell yourself, if you are honest enough. You can feel it, and if the feel-good feeling is not radiating out of your eyes and if you can't feel it in your toes, then it's not real.

So you need to find, and then practise tuning into, this feeling. How is it done? And how do you deal with other, less desirable feelings that may arise in between? How it's done is dealt with below, and transforming the less desirable feelings will be dealt with under 'Leaks and Blocks' in Part II of this book.

First you must contain the feeling

First off, you need to acknowledge that whatever money, or possessions, or dream, or goal you may be after, you are actually only after the way you think that thing is going to make you *feel*. So find that feeling. Are you wanting to feel secure, independent, powerful, free, glamorous, beautiful, content, at peace? What feeling are you after? And if you don't know, or cannot imagine, or cannot enter into feeling it, then you cannot contain it, as you do not have the shape of your container. This is all a little like those Russian dolls – a container within a container. If you cannot feel it, you cannot have it. Without strong feeling, there will be insufficient glue to hold your wealth container together, so it will probably fall apart over time, or never come together in the first place.

You will notice that I started off talking about feeling good and I am now talking about strong feelings, because the truth of it is that any strong emotion will do. We hear of people driven by determination, anger, revenge, even hate, and they succeed in their chosen quest, because the strong emotion is there. Strong emotion, of whatever kind, is energy, and it's the energy we are after.

Success is getting what you want, happiness is wanting what
you get
Unknown Wise Person

Of course this is a nice book, giving good and nice advice, to good and nice people, so having pointed out that little detail, we will continue to talk about 'feeling good' as the emotion we are after. It is also easier to work with feel-good energy as it is lighter and therefore less of a strain on the system. This way, you'll be less likely to die of a heart attack once you have achieved your goal. There is also the added advantage that tuning in to light, invigorating, feel good feelings will make you feel . . . well . . . *good*, and as like attracts like, whatever feeling you put out there with your mock-up picture of the future you, *that* is the feeling that you will move towards experiencing.

So first find out what that feeling is. It is sometimes easier to do this through association. You may recall a time and place, or even just a moment in your life, when you felt that fabulous feeling. Think back on that time and really enter into the moment. Yes, right now, wherever you are. No one needs to know. You don't have to close your eyes. Keep pretending to read the book . . . but (instead of focusing on the words) concentrate, think back to a time, place, or moment when you felt fabulous – light, energised, full of promise and anticipation. Re-experience those emotions now, and locate where it is in your body that you feel those feelings. Notice how and where the feeling spreads.

Practise this as often as you can, until you can call up the feeling without the thought, simply by directing your attention to where the feeling starts in the body, and setting up the sequence. You can also try singing, thinking of something that really excites you, *anything* in fact that will cause you to consciously raise your frequency.

> *First thoughts have tremendous energy.*
> *It is the way the mind first flashes on something*
> Natalie Goldberg in *Writing Down The Bones*

Smile and the world smiles with you

Smiling is also a good trigger. I start with the eyes, widening them and smiling with them. They in turn pull up the corners of my mouth into a smile which breathes out into my chest and heart, as I breathe out as well. It then spreads through my stomach warmly, only then do I get a sunny picture of the countryside, with me leaping up in the air. Find your happy emotion trigger. Practise using it. Use it.

Emotion is the glue that holds the material of our container together. It is the water that binds the clay or dough. And water has always been symbolically aligned with emotions. If you don't have enough, the clay won't come together. If you have too much the shape won't hold, and your container will flop.

Reflect on your life from this perspective for a moment, lightly and without judgement. How is your life held together? Is it falling apart? Or is it maybe just not coming together properly? Do you need to connect to your passion? Or do you need to let go of an emotion that no longer serves you? Reflect on what holds your wealth together emotionally? How do you hold on to your money? What holds you together?

You can process emotions over a piece of clay or flour and water. If you do it with attention and intention, you will be surprised at the results.

Putting it all together

We have looked at the material a container is made of in terms of flexibility and being a protective barrier, like skin. We said the material must be strong and dependable, and we linked this to keeping one's word and cultivating the will. We also looked at emotion as the glue that holds the material of the container together, as well as a beacon to attract what you want to you. We reflected, processed, and paid attention to our own skin, to our will, and we tightened up on our dependability and decision making.

Another aspect of a container, which is naturally related to the material it is made of, being akin to skin and boundary, is the container walls.

> *There is one thing stronger than all the armies in the world,*
> *and that is an idea whose time has come.*
> Victor Hugo

6

The Walls of Your Wealth Container

How are you containing the wealth inside your life?

Another brick in the wall

The walls of your container will determine what will go in and what will stay out of your life and your wealth journey. Walls are about your parameters and boundaries with the world and also with yourself. Without clear boundaries not only do you not know where your container begins and ends, you also can never know whether you have what you want. If you keep shifting your parameters, your walls will always be unsteady. If your walls keep getting higher and higher your container will never be full. If your walls are too thick, nothing will get through, if your walls are too thin, everything will rush through and the strain will make them collapse.

If your walls are not solid and sturdy enough, they will not hold the container together. In fact one could say that a container is nothing more than two sets of walls – the side walls and the top and bottom walls. The side walls relate to your relationship with the world around you. The bottom relates to your grounding or relationship with the earth (which we will cover under the 'base' section), and the top relates to your connection to spirit or to allowing things to flow to you (which we will cover under the 'top' section).

So we have clear boundaries, appropriate thickness, and containment because, of course, the major purpose of walls is to contain both the container and its contents. Without walls there is no container, there isn't even an incomplete container as there would be without a proper base. Because the minute you have walls (after selecting a shape), you already have something. The ground, or whatever is beneath the walls – a table or piece of wood, say, can serve as a base, though this is not the best idea. Nonetheless, you can get by without a base for a while, if you have walls and a shape.

Seeing what's on the inside

Walls are like your body; they house the inside and keep it safe. If in good condition they keep you mobile (in the case of our money container we are thinking of upwardly mobile . . .). They separate you from the world or, in other words, they define where you end and others begin. Walls determine and demarcate boundaries.

> . . . *the diffrense between a person and an angel, is that most*
> *of a person is on the*
> *inside, and most of an angel is on the outside . . .*
> from *Mister God this is Anna* by Fynn

In terms of containing money, the walls, firstly, represent making a decision. The decision is what you will have inside and what you will leave outside your container. So this is where you will be exercising choice. There are many aspects to this choice. The first and most obvious one is your choice with regard to the shape of the container itself. That is the choice you made when you decided on

59

a specific container shape – your money goal, your vision, destination, feeling, and new beingness. This was covered under the section 'The shape of your container'. This specific goal as destination was closely linked to a new you. So there was the choice to be made regarding who this new you would be and how that would feel and these both impacted on the material your container is made of.

What will you commit to, to follow your dream?

Having made these choices, having taken these decisions, the walls of your container represent a commitment to carry the vision through, because up to this point all we have is planning. Once we start building walls, there's no turning back. The walls of your container represent your commitment to exercising your choice. And this is where some of the other aspects of choice come into it, because you now need to choose your parameters and boundaries.

Now you need to decide what goes in and what stays out of your container. What are you letting go of, and what are you keeping? Because in order to execute your dream, you must change. And to change, you must transform certain elements, events, situations, and aspects of your life. You must empty out, let go of the old and the no longer useful to make space for the new – which we will cover in the section on 'fullness'.

But at this stage we are simply drawing up our parameters and choosing what will be in and what will be out. On the most simplistic levels we are possibly looking at the need to get up earlier in the morning, or perhaps we have to find the time to check or do our books if we are in business and looking to go to the next level. What we are doing is observing, and putting our intent out there for what we want changed. We are making a choice. We are saying things like, 'If I want the new wealthy me to be radiantly healthy, I may need to start an exercise programme'; 'If I want to reach my goal of owning a yacht, I may need to learn about sailing.'

Maybe I need to swap my golf club for the yacht club, because I do not have time for both. These are tough decisions, which is why most people get no further than wishing for wealth. If you are serious about your quest, however, you need to define your parameters. And you may need to make some hard choices. That's where the proper use of will comes in handy.

One of my friends gets up at 4h00 (that's in the morning) at least once a week, sometimes more often than that, to fly to business appointments. He is not a morning person, he does not like doing this, but he does it anyway. He chooses to do it because he is committed to his wealth creation plan. Part of his plan is to expand his business and part of that requires that he fly at ridiculous times of the day, so he has had to let go of sleeping in.

> *Great minds have purposes, others have wishes*
> Washington Irving

'Paying the price'

Many people see the exercising of choice and the proper use of will as 'paying the price'. If you adopt this viewpoint (even through just saying these words), your world, your container, your very heart starts to contract. Who came *up* with such garbage, anyway?

No! Expansion through skilful, intelligent, well-considered choice is a way of making your world and container more stable, and more real; it is a way of expanding. Showing commitment to the creation of a new you not only strengthens the walls of your container, it also raises your ceiling of limitation.

The ceiling is not really there

Which brings us to comfort zone. To expand from one level to another means going into discomfort or going out of your comfort zone. I attended a self-development course many years ago where several people were simply not prepared to move out of their comfort zone, to the point that they left the course halfway in a huff rather than face the challenge of doing this. And they hadn't been asked to try fire walking, merely to memorise and repeat poetry! Let's face it, if you won't stretch yourself on a course to sweat over a bit of poetry, what will you do in real life when you have a deadline that requires you work through a night (or two) to meet it? You all know the answer to that one by now, because . . . *all together now* . . . Yes! How you do anything is how you do everything! *Bravo!*

So let me say it right now. If you are not prepared to experience some discomfort, if you are not prepared to get out of your comfort zone and stretch yourself – not once but many times – then *you may as well take up embroidery or ham curing!*

If you are not ready and willing to do *whatever it takes,* which means getting right out, way out, far out of your comfort zone, then stop kidding yourself and give it up now. In all the stories of success, no matter how big or small, you will notice an absolutely unmistakable detail, and that is that at some point, and usually it's at many points, the achiever had to get right out of their comfort zone. That's what growing by definition means.

All achievers, creators, inventors, sportsmen and women, writers, entrepreneurs, healers and wealth creators who want to raise themselves to a new level have to break through some level of resistance before they can arrive at a new platform of being. It's what all the fairy tales and vision quests and heroes' journeys are all about. It's what the wealth journey is all about. It's about becoming more, having more, and raising the limits – which absolutely cannot happen if you are doing the same thing, in the same way. In fact one of the definitions of insanity is 'doing the same thing but expecting different results'.

I have met many people over the years who want to stay comfortable. They don't want to do too much, or work too hard, or miss surfing on Fridays, but they *do* want to become rich while doing these same things, in the same way, with the same outlook and attitude they have held for years, which has not been producing enough money to live on.

'How can I achieve it?' they ask. 'How can I change everything about my life without changing a thing?'

'No, I cannot answer that question,' I tell them.

Eish! (That's an African exclamation meaning something like you-gotta-be-joking-you-are-not-*seriously*-suggesting-this-are-you?)

Getting out of your comfort zone means change and that will mean different things to different people. The discomfort is not always linked to hard work or the physical, though certainly some hard work is definitely required, make no mistake. It is good to be ready and willing for that. The harder part of the journey relates to the internal changes that one has to embrace. The psychic tension of reaching new levels of being is immense. Letting go of old ideas and taking on new beliefs can be very painful for the ego. Some people will do anything rather than change their mind. Even stay miserable! *Eish!*

To recap: We were saying that walls determine what is in and what stays out of a container. They are your boundaries. And they represent choice. Choice of destination, beingness, and the choice of what forms part of your new reality and what does not. Some of this choice will be voluntary, some of it will be a compromise, a necessity or an exchange. Either way, the choice is necessary for you to grow to the next level, and for your container to have proper walls.

> *In order to get to the fruit of the tree, you have to go*
> *out on a limb*
> Shirley MacLaine

In the following processes you will contemplate your ideal life, and begin the process of defining your parameters through free writing around what you would like inside and outside the new reality you are creating. You will also set up the energetic path of attainment of this new reality through simple ceremonies that facilitate the closing off of old spaces and the opening up of new ones.

If you cannot take the time to do this processing now, read through the questions and prompts and spend a few moments contemplating each one. Then read on and return to the processing at a later date. Remember to come back!

Containing my Ideal Life
Wealth Training Process

> *Before you start, STATE YOUR INTENT! Be clear and specific. For example:*
> **'It is my intent that this processing will release the flow of wealth in my life and I am able to contain it.'**
> *Keep your pen moving*
> *Write without thinking*

Repeat the prompt if you are stuck
Keep it light!

Think for a moment of you in your ideal wealthy life, having achieved your destination and, without thinking too hard and in a free and easy, light, almost distracted way, allow your future you to answer the following questions. Spend two minutes writing on each. If you cannot write at present, reflect on the questions anyway. Daydream. It's good for you.

Allow what emerges to emerge, uncensored. No one will see this. Allow yourself the right to be totally honest. You can burn the paper later.

Another note on free writing is to be real and specific. Do not write platitudes, generalisations, or clever words that avoid the point and are basically meaningless. For example, deciding to 'enter the discomfort of a new me' is obvious but meaningless. 'Re-evaluate my present relationships' is a start, but then you need to get specific. Relationship with whom? What about them do you need to re-evaluate? And so on. Keep it REAL.

Write for two minutes on each prompt.

To live my ideal wealthy life I need to:
- Let go of ....
- Transform my ....
- Re-evaluate the/my ....
- Stop believing ....
- Enter the discomfort of ....
- Create a new..........
- Believe that ....
- Embrace ....
- Forget ....
- Re-create ....

Underline significant words or phrases with a different coloured pen, then summarise into one sentence.

Let's take a closer look at your container walls in terms of what is inside and what will be outside these walls.

Outside the Walls of My Container
Wealth Training Process

> *Before you start, STATE YOUR INTENT! Be clear and specific. For example:*
> > **'It is my intent that this processing will release the flow of wealth in my life and I am able to contain it.'**
> *Keep your pen moving*
> *Write without thinking*
> *Repeat the prompt if you are stuck*
> *Keep it light!*

Free write for two minutes on each prompt.
- The walls of my container are there to keep out ....
- Outside the walls of my container I will leave ....
- The people I know who will be outside the walls are ....
  because ....
- The people I do not know who will be outside the walls are ....
  because ....
- The belief systems I will leave outside my container walls are ....
- The emotions I will leave outside my container walls are ....
- The attitudes I will leave outside my container walls are ....
- The habits I will leave outside my container walls are ....
- The me I will leave outside my container is ....

Underline significant words or phrases with a different coloured pen, then summarise into one sentence.

Also write a list of the nine **most important words** that you want outside your container.

Here is a sample of some simple letting-go ceremonies that you can do once you have completed the writing above. A ceremony will facilitate letting go of the above. You can choose any ceremony you like, or you can make up your own. It does not matter what you do, what matters is the sincere and focused intent of your actions. Your intent here is to let go of all things that do not belong inside your container. You can refer to your container in a general way (which is best when you start) or you can be more specific and talk of your wealth container. Also remember to check the instructions for ceremonies in 'The Basics – Symbolic Acts'.

Sample Ceremonies for Letting Go
Wealth Training Process

- Take the paper you have written all of the above on, and tear it up with the intent that all that you do not want inside your container walls is no longer a part of your world. Throw the paper away. Say 'it is done', and wash your hands, symbolically 'washing your hands' of the matter.
- Burn the paper, scattering the ashes to the four winds. As you watch the ashes blow away, imagine everything you do not want inside your container blown away with them. Say 'it is done', and wash your hands. Ensure you are scattering totally dry ashes over water or sand or rock – do not start a fire.
- Bury the paper in a spot significant to you, or under a tree. Let your intent be that what you no longer want or need acts to fertilise the growth of what you do want. You can also do this with a pot plant you have bought for this purpose. Bless the spot, or tree or plant and thank it.
- Draw a circle on a piece of paper, outside the circle write all you want to let go of, inside the circle write your name. Dispose of the paper in any of the ways described above.

Now you are ready to look at what you *do* want *inside* your container. You may need first to take a break. The work you have just done is very powerful, and very tiring for most people. You have just reshuffled your psyche. This takes a lot of energy. However, at the same time, letting go of what no longer serves also creates a lot of energy. I would recommend that you take a break here, before continuing with the next section. Letting go of things can also bring on a cold or flu as well as a bout of runny tummy. This is the body's way of letting go and doing a spring clean of its own. So do not be alarmed. Everything is connected, remember!

Inside the Walls of My Container
Wealth Training Process

Free write for two minutes on each prompt.
> *Before you start, STATE YOUR INTENT! Be clear and specific.*
> *For example:*
>> **'It is my intent that this processing will release the**
>> **flow of wealth in my life and I am able to contain it.'**
> *Keep your pen moving*
> *Write without thinking*
> *Repeat the prompt if you are stuck*
> *Keep it light!*

- The walls of my container are there to keep in ....
- Inside my container I will only allow ....
- The people I know whom I will invite inside the walls are ....
- The people I do not know who will be invited inside my walls are ....
- The belief systems I will entertain inside my container walls are ....
- The emotions I will nourish inside my container walls are ....
- The attitudes I will cultivate inside my container walls are ....
- The new habits I will create inside my container walls are ....
- The new me growing inside my container will look like ....
- The new me flourishing inside my container will act like ....
- The new me living inside my container will feel like ....
- The wealth in my container will look like ....

Underline significant words or phrases with a different coloured pen, then summarise into one sentence.
Also write a list of the nine ***most important words*** that you want inside your container.

Once you have completed the above writing, you may want to perform some simple ceremony to open up a new space for all the new aspects of your life that you want to contain in your container. Here are a few samples. You can choose any ceremony you like, or you can make up your own. It does not matter what you do, what matters is the sincere and focused intent of your actions. Your intent here is to create the space in your life and your container for all those things you want in it. You can refer to your container in a general way (which is best when you start) or you can be more specific and talk of your wealth container.

Sample Ceremonies for Opening Up a New Space
Wealth Training Process

- Write each of the elements you want inside your container on a separate piece of paper. Make, or buy, or find in your home, a beautiful bowl, or jug, or vase, or chalice to be your symbolic container. Create a quiet space. Light a candle. Add some scent or music if you like. With focused and respectful intent, invite the elements you want in your container into your life and into your container, as you read them out one by one and place them inside your chalice. Give thanks at the end. You may want to keep your chalice in a special place in your home.
- Have a dance party, using music with a beat rather than ethereal wind-type music. Dance and celebrate the arrival of each of the elements you want in your container by calling them out one by one from a prepared list. Imagine you are one of those fancy butlers at a gala occasion announcing the arrival of royalty. As you call out each element ground it into your life and container by stamping your feet to the beat.
- Do a combination of dance and chalice by dancing and then placing each element written individually on paper, into a chalice after being called out.
- Draw a circle on a big piece of paper. Inside the circle write your name and all the elements you want inside your container. You may want to colour or illustrate the paper. Put it up somewhere where you can see it regularly, until you no longer need to see it.
- Celebrate! Prepare to receive!

There are two things to aim at in life: first to get what you want; and after that, to enjoy it.
Only the wisest of mankind achieve the second
Leonardo Parmigiani

What you have accomplished through this processing is a powerful transformation of your wealth container. You have started creating and firming your container walls. Against the backdrop of your ideal life, which you have begun to create, you have initiated the process of differentiation. You uncovered and released some of the things you are not prepared to have inside your new container and life. You impressed this intent upon the universe through focusing your will in ceremony. You also opened up a new space energetically, and named those things you *do* want inside your container. Your walls are forming. You, your wealth, and your life are transforming! *Well done!*

In the next chapter we will look at container walls in terms of their function as boundary and parameter.

7

Boundaries and Parameters

If you won't draw the line, who will?

Drawing the line

Let's go back to the walls. In the previous chapter we looked at what walls keep in and out of your container; now let's look at the walls themselves. Walls, as we said before, represent your commitment to honouring your choice of what to have inside and what to keep outside your container. What will enable you, and the walls, to honour this commitment are your boundaries and parameters. So we will look at those now.

Boundaries are borders. Boundaries are a space between things, a no-man's-land, a neutral space, a space of rest. Boundaries dictate where one thing ends and another begins, they demarcate the personal space of self and of others. Respecting this neutral space of others and expecting one's own neutral space to be respected is what boundaries are all about.

Boundaries relate to situations as well as to people and they certainly are a key aspect in the process of containing money. If your boundaries with the world are unclear it will affect, first and foremost, your communication. It will also affect your decision making and your ability to act. Quite simply, a boundary is the difference between this and that and if you cannot tell that difference, then you are really in trouble.

There are many reasons that people have boundary issues. Lack of the ability to confront is the main one. Inability to confront means inability to say what you want or mean, which is also inability to say 'no', which will naturally result in all sorts of complication and confusion.

Learning to say 'no' is one of the most crucial skills you can cultivate in life. Little children have no problem saying no. I ask my five-year-old if she wants to go and play with a friend and she may well say, 'No, I don't want to play with him any more.' Just like that. Even though they have played together almost weekly for months, now she doesn't want to. I try to rationalise, offer compromise and she still says no. Her boundaries are clear. She will not be moved.

I remember a friend complaining one day because an insurance salesman was coming to see her. She did not have the time; moreover, she had an insurance broker; she did not need more insurance, but she couldn't say no to the appointment on the phone. I wondered how she would say no to the salesman face to face (which she assured me she would do) when she could not bring herself to say no to an appointment on the telephone.

How many things have you bought or done or said because you just couldn't say no? (Everyone is allowed one of *those* nights out, so that doesn't count.) Every time you say 'yes' when you mean 'no' you weaken your boundaries, or the walls of your container. Every time you say 'yes', when you want to say 'no' you weaken your will and your resolve and the power of your word.

And she said, 'Let it be so!' and it was so . . .

When you weaken your word you not only weaken your walls, you also weaken the material of your container – you make it runny and soft. When that happens, your container loses its shape. When you weaken your word, your word has no power. When your word has no power, you cannot call what you want to you, or banish what you do not want. When you cannot keep your word, you cannot rely on or depend on or trust yourself and then you will feel the same way about others too. And then, as like attracts like, they will come to you to show you their lack of trust and their lack of dependability, and you will feel hard done by, and not very powerful, and not very able to accomplish your dreams.

When your boundaries are weak because you cannot say what you mean, then you pour yourself out into the personal space of others, as you will not respect their parameters if you do not respect your own. So you will do and say inappropriate things. You will be the body therapist who phones her clients at all sorts of hours to discuss her man problems – lack of boundaries. You will be that mind therapist who tells his clients about his own problems during sessions instead of holding the space for theirs – lack of boundaries. You will be the client who phones her fund manager at the weekend or late at night at home to discuss her investments – lack of boundaries.

Say what you mean, and mean what you say

I believe it all starts with the basic inability to say that little word 'NO'. We are encouraged to say 'yes', to agree, to acquiesce, to comply, to obey. Especially as children, we are conditioned to believe that this is a good thing and 'no' in all its forms is not a good thing. We learn early that we are expected to please. We are expected to please everyone – our parents, teachers, friends, society, partners, even total strangers. And linked to this expectation to please is the need to feel accepted and liked. Most adults seem to need everyone to like and approve of them. Everyone! How crazy and unrealistic is that? And so to ensure this happens, we never say 'no'. The five-year-old phase of being able to say 'no' quite comfortably does not last long. Once we get into the habit of pleasing, it's a downward spiral. Women in particular have been encouraged, even instructed, simply to please.

SAY NO TO THAT!

SAY NO! RIGHT NOW!

It's not just women who cannot say 'no'. Men, even powerful men in powerful positions, suffer from this condition. It may express itself differently, but it's the same condition. Whereas the woman might book an appointment with the salesman because she cannot say 'no', the businessman may simply avoid speaking to him. He tells his secretary he will not take the call, or he keeps telling the salesman he is busy, and will get back to him. Both are low confront techniques. Both reflect an inability to express clearly. Both express an inability to say 'no'.

Stand with your 'nos' held high!

When you can say 'no', clearly and firmly, you are holding your own space – which is what we are talking about here. When you can hold your space, you are standing firmly, like the walls of your container – straight up and strong. Not only that, but when you can say 'no' you will also be able to tolerate others saying 'no' to you without crumbing and falling apart.

How many things have you avoided doing, confronting, dealing with, approaching, opening up, beginning, ending, continuing or overcoming simply because you were too scared to hear someone say that little word 'no' to you?

REFLECT on that for a moment.

And now, reflect on the following:

- How many opportunities have you allowed to pass by?
- How much wealth have you closed the door to?
- How many potential sales, wins, clients, business deals, have you let slip through your fingers because you were so very, very, scared of even *the possibility* of encountering that little word 'no'.

Look at it: such a tiny, tiny, little word to be afraid of   No

It's even scarier when we think its *final*   No

And when someone is really committed, like   No!
It becomes some kind of   NOOOOOOOOOHHHH!!!!!!!!
in our minds. And we run!

What makes a winner is the ability to go beyond NO
Kiki Theo

Stand up tall and straight. Let your walls be firm. Learn to say 'no', clearly and firmly. Open yourself to the possibility of hearing 'no' from others and still standing tall. Sometimes the 'no' means maybe, sometimes it is a paving stone to 'yes'. Sometimes it's just 'no'. Respect the 'nos' of others. Be clear on your parameters and where you draw the line. Know what you are saying 'no' to. This brings in issues of honour and keeping your word, and ethics.

You need to know where you stand, and you need to be able to stand firm and tall because making money will test you. It will test your walls, your will, and your parameters. You need to know where you stand. Some of the lessons you need to learn will only be revealed to you at the time, under pressure and under duress. And, yes, you will be tempted, sorely tempted, by many tantalising things waving to you at the end of murky means, once you commit to your wealth journey. You don't need to take the murky roads. You definitely do not. I don't care how much you've heard that getting dirty in business is the only way to get ahead. It is not. Getting dirty is an option and a choice like everything else in life. No one forces you to take this choice, and if you've taken it you cannot blame anyone but yourself.

Let's do some processing on saying 'no' and on parameters.

Ninety percent of my money I intend to spend on wild women,
booze, and good
times, and the other ten percent I will spend foolishly
Tug McGraw

In the processing that follows you will enter into intensive and powerful definition, and redefinition of your parameters. You will reflect on your boundaries with respect to others, as well as on the effect that the boundaries of others have upon you. You will reformat and re-pattern some habitual behaviour around boundaries and execute inspired action to change parameters which no longer serve you.

If you are unable to do this processing now, skip forward and come back to it at a later time or date. But do come back! This is very important and crucial processing for this work!

Defining My Parameters
Wealth Training Process

Write for three minutes on each prompt. Allow what emerges to emerge. Let your pen write. Repeat the prompt if you become stuck. Please note that prompts are ambiguous and generalised for a reason. Write according to what the prompt means to you.

(**Important note**: If you have ever been involved in any form of physical coercion, please do not process this here. These exercises are meant to deal with parameters, boundaries and issues around the ability to confront with regard to day-to-day dealings with people and everyday situations. These processes are not meant to deal with traumatic events which should be processed with the help of a professional. If the questions elicit responses to do with traumatic events, you can set up your parameters at the start and choose not to deal with traumatic events in these exercises. *(Do see a professional to deal with trauma in a safe environment.)*

> *Before you start, STATE YOUR INTENT! Be clear and specific. For example:*
> > **'It is my intent that this processing will release the flow of wealth in my life and I am able to contain it.'**
> *Keep your pen moving*
> *Write without thinking*
> *Repeat the prompt if you are stuck*
> *Keep it light!*

1. My parameter is ....
2. Where I draw the line is ....
3. List

(a) Five situations (one sentence each) where others regularly invade your boundaries.

Be specific about the person and the incident.

Example 1. My mother insists on feeling me to see if I am wearing a bra.

(b) Your usual response to each one.

Example 1. I regress to being a child, giggle and push her away.

(c) Create and decide on a new response that keeps your boundaries strong.

Example 1. I will say 'No', fold my arms over my chest, tell her I will no longer allow this.

(d) Execute your decision.

4. List

(a) Five situations (one sentence each) where you regularly invade the boundaries of others. Be specific about the person and the incident.

Example 2. I use humour to attack John and make him feel small.

(b) Your thoughts and feelings around the person and the incident.

Example 2. John makes 'funny', but belittling comments about my career. He makes me feel small; my response to him makes me feel powerful.

(c) Create and decide on a new response that keeps boundaries in place.

Example 2. I will tell John that I find his jokes about my career unpleasant and ask him to stop. If he persists, I will simply say 'No, I don't find that funny,' and walk away. (What's 'my career' in this example? Well, this is an example, so you can use your imagination. It could be anything from a professional belly dancer, to a cartoonist or even a dog walker.)

(d) Execute your decisions.

5. List

(a) Five areas around which your parameters are always tested.

(b) Three ways in which you can transform each one.

(c) Execute.

6. List your three most important parameters around each of the following areas of life. Be very specific. You may wish first to free write on each aspect, and then underline and extract the most important parameters.
    (a) Work
    (b) Money making
    (c) Family
    (d) Friends
    (e) Strangers
    (f) Love relationships
    (g) Fun and Play
    (h) Self – body, mind, spirit, emotions (do each separately)
    (i) Eating
    (j) Personal space
    (k) Commitments
    (l) Goals
7. (a) What do you consider a serious breach of parameters? List your top ten.
    (b) Decide and commit to never allowing these to form a part of your reality, but phrase these intentions positively.
        For example if 'having garlic breath breathed close to me'is a no-no for you (look ma, *two 'no's*), commit to 'Allowing only those with fresh clean breath near my nose'. Also commit to never breaching these parameters with others.
8. How many of these breaches do you allow on a regular basis?
    (a) If not already dealt with in 3 or 4 above, use the framework provided in 3 and 4, to define, analyse and create a positive change with regard to these incidents.
    (b) Decide now that you will maintain your parameters and boundaries.
    (c) Execute your decisions.

Look with thine ears
William Shakespeare

Celebrate! Congratulate yourself! Write about what you have achieved and what has changed in the way you deal with people and situations as well as in the way you feel. Wait a month and then review where you are again. Celebrate again! You can never celebrate enough! Acknowledge your wins and transformation! Give thanks!

A warrior must only take care that his spirit is never broken
Shissai

What you have accomplished

Not only have you raised your ability to confront significantly, but you have tightened your parameters and boundaries. You have consciously decided what your parameters are. And you have listed these requirements for every area of your life. You have increased your ability to say what you mean and to say 'no'. In other words, you have strengthened your parameters and the walls of your container.

You are now aware of the importance of maintaining your boundaries as well as of respecting the boundaries of others. You have your attention on the correct use of your word and of your will. This means you are building good strong walls to contain your wealth.

Bravo! Well done!

Below, you will find a fantastic Advanced Wealth Process called 'Raising your ability to confront – saying No' which will take you to the next level in your processing around parameters. Do this process in about a week or two's time, depending on the effect the previous processing has had on you.

Do not get psychic or emotional or mental indigestion. Take your time to absorb!

Chew slowly and nicely!

When you reach real ability you will be able to become one with the enemy. Entering his heart you will see that he is not your enemy after all
Tsuji – Japanese sword master

Raising Your Ability to Confront – Saying 'No'
Advanced Wealth Processing

1. List eleven incidents when you wanted to say 'no' and did not. Re-

play each incident in your head and say 'no', as well as anything else you need to say.

2. List eleven incidents when you did not say what you meant. Write down what you should have said for each one. Replay the incident in your head with the words you should have said.

3. List three situations which occur regularly, where you do not say what you mean. Decide to say what you mean. Do it.

4. List three situations where you did not say, or do, what you wanted to. Rectify the situation. Do this again as many times as necessary.

5. Look for three situations coming up in the near future where you would normally not say 'no', even though you want to. Plan to say 'no'. Do it.

6. See whether you can say 'no' to something every day for a week, just for practice.

7. List seven things you have been putting off doing because of some unpleasantness linked to the item. Do them. Repeat as necessary.

8. List seven things you feel uncomfortable doing. Do one each day of the week and repeat the list each week for a month, or until you are no longer uncomfortable with the item. You can repeat with more items, and/or increase the severity of discomfort. Do not put yourself in any danger!

If you have completed all the previous exercises, you should be feeling Strong, Powerful, Grounded, and Balanced!

Channel this energy into something constructive and positive in the real world that will help to advance your dreams. Always channel positive energy created in processing into something concrete in the world.

Well done!

Are you ready for more? Let's look a little bit at the thickness of your walls. Although this is closely linked to parameters, the thickness of your container walls is not determined by parameters alone.

8

The Thickness of the Walls of Your Container

How can wealth get through to you?

Is your wealth only skin deep?

The thickness or thinness of your walls is affected by parameters, the material of your container, your attitude and faith. If the walls around you, or your container, or your life, or your wealth are too thick, nothing will enter. If they are too thin, everything will collapse. What does this mean, especially with regard to money? And what does attitude and faith have to do with it?

It's simply this. If your walls are too thick, like armour around you, then everything – people, fortuitous events, wealth, luck – will be kept away. This armour is predominantly an attitude. You know those people who have a go-away-and-leave-me-alone (see, I am maintaining the parameters of nice language here) sign across their foreheads? Do you go near them? Are you drawn towards them at all? And those people who are closed and dark and secretive, do you invite them to share in your new moneymaking plans? Do they make you feel you can trust them? And what about the thin-walled types, the blabbering, talkative, can't-keep-a-secret, in-everyone's-business types? Do you go to them with your new invention that will revolutionise the world and make a fortune?

And if you were money, this great expansive energy, would you feel comfortable in a container where the walls are so thick they crush you and there is little space for you to fit in or breathe? Or could you be contained by a container with walls so flimsy that the next wind could blow them down?

Contemplate and reflect upon how thick or thin the walls around you are in life and also in business. Are you open to new ideas, new ways of doing things, the possibility that you can change, that your fortunes can change? Or are you like a crab, or a tortoise, with a thick shell around you, unwilling to let anything in? Because one thing is for absolute certain: to go from where you are, to where you want to be means, by definition, change. If you are not willing to change, you can go nowhere – not even into your bath (I am soooo funny today!). But it's true!

So, how do you cultivate the right texture of container walls? Well, fortunately, as we know, everything is connected. We also know that it is probably easier to work with a piece of clay than with our minds, which are notoriously unruly and recalcitrant. So, I would recommend building a container – you can use the very simple method described earlier. All you need is time, a quiet space and the right intent. Give yourself at least one hour. I usually give people two. State your intent to shift your attitude, or to become more flexible, or to create the most appropriate thickness for your walls. Then begin to create a container with special attention to the walls. Observe without judgement when you are done. Repeat when you are drawn to do so.

The mere acknowledgement and desire to change something is actually the start of that process. State what you want to change. Trust that the change will happen.

Besides that, the wealth trainings you are doing around parameters and material and attitude will radically transform and adjust the thickness of your container walls. Just add your awareness of thickness to that.

Some things are simply very short and sweet – like this chapter. When they are, we just say, *The End.*

9

The Base of Your Container

What supports your wealth vision?

On the ground

The base of your container represents your grounding and your support. When you create a container – as has been suggested in various places above – whether it is drawn or created out of clay or dough, examine its base. In fact, you will learn all you need to know about the condition of your symbolic container (and also about the state of your wealth) through the simple observation of the container that you draw or create. All the answers are there if you observe with an open mind, and if you use the clues and reflections provided in this book.

So have a look at the base of the container you drew way back at the beginning. Does it even have a base? Is the base in proportion to the rest of the container? In other words, is the base so small that the container will topple? Does it make the container unstable? Will the base hold your container, balance it and keep it grounded?

These are all different ways of saying: is there support, and is there grounding? And what exactly do those words mean? Well, they mean many things, as always. Support talks of general support for your goal or idea, for your dream. Is there support for it from those near and dear, from the world, from your prospective clients? In terms of a general container of life and of self, the question is a general, 'are you supported?' and you will know what that means to you and whether you are or not. So let's look at the idea of support for a moment.

If you cannot do this processing now, read each prompt and reflect on it for a few moments. Then read on, but remember to return here and do the processing properly at a later time or date.

Support
Wealth Training Process

Free write for two minutes on each prompt.

Allow what emerges to emerge. Let your pen write. Repeat the prompt if you become stuck. Please note that prompts appear ambiguous and generalised for a reason. Write according to what the prompt means to you.

> *Before you start, STATE YOUR INTENT! Be clear and specific. For example:*
> **'It is my intent that this processing will release the flow of wealth in my life and I am able to contain it.'**
> *Keep your pen moving*
> *Write without thinking*
> *Repeat the prompt if you are stuck*
> *Keep it light!*

- I see support as ....
- The support in my life has always come from ....
- What I am supported on in life is ....

- What I am not supported on in life is ....
- The person/people who support me the most are ....
- The person/people who give me the least support are ....
- Generally, I feel supported/unsupported (choose) and this makes me feel ....
- The way I can increase support in my life is ....
- I have support for wealth creation from ....
- The person who would most disapprove of my creating wealth is .... because .... and this makes me feel ....and then what I do is ....
- The way I give support to others is ....
- The person/people I give support to in my life are .... because ....
- The things I support most are ....
- The person/people I give no support to in my life are .... because ....
- I support the process of wealth creation through ....
- Wealth supports ....
- The universe supports ....

Underline important or significant words and phrases in a different coloured pen. Summarise into one sentence.

I will always cherish the initial misconceptions I had about you
Unknown Wise Person

'But Mummy has to approve'

As you were doing this exercise, and now, as you read over what you have written, I am sure you discovered some pretty amazing things. I am also sure you saw a link or relationship between the way you support (or not) and the way you are supported (or not). This is a wonderful thing, because it means that you can change the way you are supported by changing the way you support. Some of you may have been surprised to discover that your support does not come from the sources you imagined, you may also have been surprised to discover that those you thought should be supporting you (sometimes those near and dear) are not, in fact, supporting

85

you at all.

This is a very common phenomenon, because the media brainwash us with pictures of the supposed 'ideal'. We all believe that parents and spouses and siblings of very nice people, in very nice families, living very nice lives, are happy and supportive, kind, and willing to help. We see people interviewed on television saying, 'Yes, I owe it all to my mother, I could never have done it without her.' And then we believe that if that is not the case in our lives, we must be the minority, so we'd better not even admit this is happening to ourselves, let alone to anyone else.

Well, the good news is that the ideal life happens mostly on television. Back here in the real world, the ideal happens to such a teensy, tiny, minority of people that it can be disregarded as a percentage. Think of all the people you know and have known in your life, for example, and then pick out the TV-perfect ideal ones. See what I mean? And if you are one of those lucky few, don't smirk – celebrate your good fortune!

We may have the situation that our nearest and dearest do not support us. The first thing to do is to confront and acknowledge this information. See it for what, and as what it is. Do not take it personally. There are many reasons why those closest and dearest, even parents, siblings or spouses do not support us in the fulfilment of our dreams. We can never know all the reasons, nor would it be of any use to us if we did. The only thing we want to be clear on is who does and who does not support us. Because if we spend our time trying to get support from those who are not only not giving it, but often are undermining our efforts, then all we are doing is shooting ourselves in the foot. Not liking the fact that others do not give us support, thinking that they should, demanding that they must, being angry and frustrated and discouraged about it will not help us to get their support. You cannot force or reason or coerce support. Support is there, or it is not. Best find out where it's not and stop trying to find it there.

You cannot contain for others

I was very fortunate to study Jung for seven years with a wonderful man who was one of my most important mentors. I met him while

I was working as a telemarketer for a fund management company which I bought some seven years later once I had started and grown my own company. As we grew more and more successful, my mentor would warn me to beware of jealousy and envy. He told me that my own family would be less than pleased at my success. He warned me to be aware and to be prepared for a certain isolation that comes with success.

Of course I heard him, but I laughed and did not take it too seriously until the day we bought a huge fancy Georgian house for our business premises. It was really so grand, especially for two little people (my partner and I) who had started a business on shoestring savings and a prayer. The entrance to the house was a long paved pathway through wonderful gardens bordered on either side with iceberg roses. We were (so) excited! We were so innocent. We really believed and expected *everyone* would be as thrilled and over the moon as we were. And guess what? My mentor had been right. And to this day, some fifteen years later, I still cannot understand why my family were not as thrilled and over the moon as I was. Their response was, to say the very least, somewhat restrained.

And out of hundreds of clients, dozens of stockbrokers, bankers, and suppliers of every kind, there were only three people who openly, honestly and unreservedly congratulated us on our achievement. That, too, I never understood, though I learnt a big lesson, a hard lesson, perhaps even a sad lesson. And that lesson is that support does not, and will not necessarily come from the people you expect it to come from.

However, I have also discovered over the years, those people (some close, some not so close) who support me and are happy to rejoice in my success. These people, whom I regard as my spiritual family, are treasured, and I feel truly grateful to have them in my life.

First you support yourself

We have been looking at support as something given by others, but support is also something we first need to give to ourselves and this is very important, especially once you've had a wake-up call like the one I have described above. This is not to say that you cut out people or become closed, relying only on yourself, because that does not help you. It is merely an awareness of what is. It is an acknowledgement of how things are and the realisation that the world may not necessarily be running around you celebrating your success. It is crucially important to know this. Once you do, you can truly appreciate those people who genuinely and unconditionally do support you, for they are really precious. You can also come to appreciate and cultivate the most consistent form of support you can ever get, which is support from within you and from the Divine.

How do you support yourself? Well, at some point you need to become your own mother and father and sister and brother and husband and wife, and if that sounds too esoteric, what it means is this – you need to become your own source of support and acknowledgement. You need to learn to say to yourself, 'Well done! That was brilliant! You were so great!' But I see some of you cringe at the mere thought of that idea, because we have been taught that that is not done. Too arrogant! Thinking too much of yourself, and so on. But let me tell you that if you cannot support yourself, how can you expect anyone else to? If you don't honestly believe that you are the absolute best person for the job, whatever that may be, how will you convince anyone else of the fact?

When I saw people about their investments, I absolutely believed that I was the very best person that they could be dealing with. I believed without a shadow of doubt that no one, I mean *no one*, would ever give them the service, and the commitment and the returns that I would. There was no doubt in my mind that I was the best person they could be dealing with. I believed this when I was selling portfolio management, power tools and wall coating. I believe it when I am coaching and when I deliver courses. I believe it of myself now, as I write books that I know everyone will benefit from and be inspired by. (And remember, as I write this, I still do not even have a single book published, let alone a positive response from an agent or publisher.[1]) Full of myself? Maybe. Confident? For sure! Believing in myself? Yes! Supporting myself? Definitely!

Supporting yourself also means taking yourself seriously. Because,

---

[1]   This is how my first draft read!

again, if you don't, who will? Taking yourself seriously means commitment. While you potter around at home with clay, you are just 'doing some clay work'. When you rent premises and get a company name and a telephone line, you are in the business of ceramics. If you take yourself seriously, so will everyone around you.

> *Approach the moment with the idea that you're in the fight*
> *to the finish*
> Mataemon Iso

Having the faith to commit

Commitment means sticking your neck out. It is 'that point between decision and action where grace can step in' (as Rashid Feild says). So support is not just a passive acknowledgement, or holding the space for possibility to unfold, it is also active in the sense that you need to take a step towards your goal.

Whereas the shape of your container represents a decision regarding your choice of a specific destination, goal, new beingness, and the cultivation of the right energy and feeling for this; and whereas your walls represent the commitment to achieve and contain that goal through the firming of your parameters and boundaries, and through further clarification of what you will allow to be inside and outside your container; and whereas the material of your container represents your ability and willingness to deliver, or your dependability; all of which are the stage of unmanifest creation, dreaming, the cocoon or seed phase; the *base* of your container is the place of early action. (Okay, even I had to read that again, slowly – but it does make sense – so go back and read it again!)

Now, I'll rephrase in more compact form:
- *Shape* – decision regarding choice of destination, goal, new beingness and cultivation of right energy and feeling.
- *Walls* – commitment to achieve and contain goal through firming parameters and boundaries – clarification of what you will allow inside and outside container.
- *Material* – ability and willingness to deliver, your dependability.
- All together are part of the unmanifest stage of creation, dream-

ing, the cocoon or seed phase; **BUT**
- ***Base*** *is the place of early action!*

This is why we talk of forming a base, or putting down foundations, or strong roots. Forming a strong base is crucial to the survival of any enterprise, whether it be an organism like self, a relationship, a family, a business or wealth.

The way you support your wealth vision, apart from believing and trusting in yourself, is through grounding that vision into reality, or forming a firm base for the dream to take root and unfold.

Many of you, especially gardeners and farmers, will tell me that the base, the roots, is where we should have started in the first place. This is only true to a point. What we have been doing until now, is creating and planting and caring for our seeds. Without knowing what you are planting, without a clear idea of which tree or flower, or orchard you want to create, it is difficult to develop a base or roots. What would you be creating a base for? But perhaps I should not be mixing my metaphors, so let's get back to the container.

First think, then do
Albert Schweitzer

Action will give you the power

How do we ground our vision? Through action. Beyond the affirmative, emotional, symbolic, and energetic levels of support, we need to look at support in a practical sense, in terms of realities such as feasibility, expenses versus income, projections, plans, and stuff your bank manager or investor will want to see. In other words, we need to test our dream against reality, just as they do with cars. Someone has an idea, then they build a magnificent something, then they run tests to see if it can withstand reality. And that is what your base or support will determine – whether your container will be able to stand up to reality.

Let's look at support in terms of these other, more realistically concrete parameters. We start off by saying that, definitely, your container must have your support, which means your commitment to make it happen, which if you don't have enough of, will cause the container to collapse – so you will know it's time to get back to the basics.

The container has your support and through your connection with the feeling at the destination of your goal and new you, you have enlisted the support of the Divine. And as like attracts like, so you are beaming a powerful energetic magnet out into the world, full of great feel-good energy and the world is responding by preparing all similar good things to come your way too.

Now, this is a general book about containing money, so I cannot go into manifestation or goal and business creation in great detail – you will have to read my books, *The Art of Conscious Creation* and *Business Alchemy* for that. But let us just say that now is the time to consider the practicalities involved in the achievement of the new wealthy you. This need not be difficult or complicated. You do not need an accountant or business strategist before you start, not at this stage, anyway. Find me a successful person who started a business because a business strategist worked out a plan for them first. It does not happen that way, not in real life, only in the banking ads and in the minds of people who have never been in business.

In real life you need to sit down and ask yourself some simple questions and then do some simple (and I mean simple) maths involving addition and subtraction – you could even use a calculator.

Here is a case scenario as an example, followed by some questions you can use on your own wealth creation dream. Remember, the simpler something is, the better. Use very basic, very simple logic. Don't get clever. Some of the most successful people are not necessarily more intelligent, but they have the ability to keep things simple, which means seeing the obvious. Seeing the obvious is a function of looking, of being totally in the present, and of seeing what is there, usually staring you in the face.

Cultivate the ability to see what is there. Cultivate the ability to see the obvious. This requires moving out of our normal, habitual mode of thinking. Great modern-day thinkers, like Edward de Bono, suggest techniques for the cultivation of the right brain – that part of the brain that is more creative and more able to execute 'lateral thinking'. I believe that these techniques enable you to cultivate being fully in the present too. And when you are, not only are both parts of your brain engaged, but you are fully in your power too. Some useful exercises are listed at the end of this section in this regard.

Meanwhile, I will illustrate what I mean by gaining the support of reality through first observing the obvious, through the following case scenario. It is one involving a business venture, but the details can be applied to anything else too.

The Pizza Parlour
A short lesson in business

Down the road from where I live there was a successful pizza parlour which was sold to a new owner. The new owner (who had bought a successful going concern) began by changing everything (which had been working). He changed the name, the menu, and the decor. From a colourful very obvious red and green chequered typical pizza parlour look (which had been working) the colours were changed to black and white. This restaurant fronts a main road opposite a busy beach, with large, floor-to-ceiling windows. The new pizza parlour opened only at night. Business was very quiet until new owner number one eventually closed a year or so later.

New owner number two took over and, keeping decor, menu and name the same (which had not been working), proceeded to do exactly what the previous owner had done (which had not been working), that is, sell pizza and open only at night. (Did I say 'which had not been working'?) He lasted a little less time than the previous owner (who had not made it work), before he, too, closed about a year later.

Can you bear to hear that this happened again? A third time? Well it did! New owner – number three – same menu, same decor, same name, still selling pizza at night, no business, close down.

So what is the problem, and how could it have been avoided? What is 'the obvious' here that was not looked at? Where is the lack of support? And remember we are working with the firm belief that we are always supported, so it's a matter of finding the support which exists in every situation. So keep one eye on that, as we run through our case scenario.

If it works, don't mess with it: If it doesn't, do

Let's look at the obvious. New owner number one had bought a successful going concern, and instead of simply continuing as everything had been before, he changed everything. This was an obvious mistake. It's a mistake I'm sure you have experienced first hand at some time in your life. Just when you find a shampoo you really like, they 'improve' the recipe and change it. Then you stop buying it. It's like buying the well-known cola label because everyone loves it and buys it, and then changing the recipe, or the name. This is obviously not a good idea. And the operative word here is 'obviously'!

Then, new owners number two and three imagined that they could do exactly the same as new owner number one (who was failing), and succeed. How is that possible? They needed to do something different. They needed to change something. Now this is not genius stuff, and you really do not need to call in a professional to point out the obvious to you.

If something is working, and you change what was making it work to something else, you cannot guarantee that it will continue to work. If something is not working, on the other hand, and you continue doing what made it not work, you can guarantee that it will continue not to work. This is very, very, simple, very, very, basic, very, very obvious logic. (Did I say very? And obvious?)

So what else is obvious in this scenario? Well, we have been talking about support, and we are looking at support in the real world, and what this means is clients. No matter what you are doing in this world you need a client. And when it comes to your wealth vision, you need to test it against the support of that client or clients in the real world. So you need to ask yourself, who are my clients in this venture, where are they, what do they want, do they want what I am offering, and why should they want what I'm offering? (The last sentence, if used correctly, can probably ensure the success of a business.) In other words, is there support for this venture?

If they are not there, they cannot buy it

Let's go back to the example, and let's look at the obvious again. Once new owner number two realises the obvious fact that he needs to change what was happening before in order to succeed, the next obvious thing to consider is that to sell anything you need people. Where are the people who will support this venture? Simple observation in the case of this particular pizza parlour shows that although the beach across the road is full of people during the day, offering loads of passing trade, it is a residential area with no traffic at night.

So the most logical, obvious, simple change to make is to open during the day, and maybe even consider closing at night. Not the other way around. The obvious is usually the observable. This is very important. Trust what you can see more than what you imagine or hope for. But, most of all, trust what you sense or intuit.

What that means is this: If you cannot see lots of people walking past your pizza parlour, don't imagine they will suddenly appear out of thin air, just because you are there. (Unless you are a world famous chef, with an extensive PR department and budget and, even then, I would be cautious.) See the obvious. The obvious here is that people are in the area in the day and not at night time. To discover this simple fact requires just looking and seeing what is there.

There are a few other obvious things to see in this example. Once you have established 'when' prospective clients or your support are around, the next thing to do is find out 'who' they are, because this will give you an idea of what they want, or buy, which again in this case you can observe simply by looking. So let's look at what the support base of clients is like.

In this example, you will observe that the beach is frequented by locals who live in the area, tourists who visit in season, and a bulk of working-class fisher folk and children who arrive in buses in their droves, especially at the weekends and in season. You will also notice that most of the people bring some sort of *bought* takeaway food to the beach – fish and chips, fried chicken and lots of cool drinks, crisps and so on. And they eat it on the beach. Need I state the obvious here?

Why not sell what they want to buy to the people who are already coming to the area, so they can eat it on the beach? Especially as *no one else is doing this*. This is an obvious conclusion from an obvious observation. All it requires is a shift in thinking, away from trying to get reality to fit in with you, to trying to accommodate the reality that already exists. In other words, use the support of gravity, don't fight against it. If the people want fish and chips, don't try to force pizza on them!

That is what I mean when I say, does reality support your vision? This is how you test whether reality supports your vision. If you can accommodate the reality around you, it in turn will support you, because everything is connected. And in fact, reality is *always* trying to support you. Believe it!

The thing about reality, the concrete observable reality that we are talking about here, is that it is real. It is what you can see and touch and hear and feel. It is quantifiable. People come undone in business ventures, in their vision, and in their container, when their ideas remain in the realm of the head, and the realm of unquantifiable speculation. New owner number three no doubt imagined that he could keep everything the same but offer 'better service', 'more tasty food', or 'work harder', or maybe even 'have a better attitude' and 'care more'. None of that is tangible. None of that addresses the support base of this venture.

So what has happened to the pizza parlour? Well, after another year of standing empty, the most recent owner has redecorated everything (AGAIN!). He has poshed it up, and is offering an eclectic menu, including very fancy pizza. They are open for lunch and dinner and I must say that although they are doing much better than anyone has in years, they are still not (in my opinion) taking full advantage of the available clientele in the area. People still bring in their own takeaway food to the beach. Most locals still eat regularly at one of the many excellent, established restaurants down the road, which brings us to my last point.

Tell me why I should buy it

We have looked at when/where the clients are, and who the clients are – in other words, who is the support? The last point I want to look at, as I raised it earlier and as I do like completing things (an important aspect of delivery), is: 'Why should clients buy what I offer, or why should they deal with me?' This, too, forms part of the support of the vision, and in our case, the container.

This is a crucial question you should be asking before embarking on any business venture. Why should the client deal with me? To answer the question properly and meaningfully requires that you put yourself in the buyer's shoes. It requires that you shift perspective from your own to that of another looking at you. And again it is an act of looking at the obvious.

The answer to this question will reveal what you have to offer that is extraordinary or, in other words, how well you know your strengths and also how well you know your market, your competitors, and your prospective clients. When we ask why someone should deal with us, it automatically presupposes that we know our market. In this case (apart from clients and their needs which we looked at earlier) this means we also know who is running the other restaurants in the area, what they have on their menus and how they are doing. And if you open up a restaurant before going out to eat at every single restaurant in your area (repeatedly), then you are doing yourself a great disservice.

In very close proximity to the ex-pizza parlour, in a pocket all of its own, which one can easily walk around, is a veritable smorgasbord of fabulous restaurants and delis to suit every taste and pocket. There are restaurants overlooking the harbour, on the very edge of the sea – spectacular views, superb food and ambience, log fires in winter. There is a deli, famous throughout Cape Town, where each dish is freshly prepared before you, on a menu that changes daily. Pastries, cakes and breads are baked daily on the premises too; the place buzzes with locals; the waiters are like family.

What you see is what you get
Flip Wilson

More choices than fish in the sea . . .

On the very edge of the sea, you can sit on an elevated wooden deck as the waves splash right against the wall and whales leap out of the water during their season. This buzzy drinking spot serves basic fish and chips, burgers, salads and great pizza. There is a wonderful boulangerie-cum-coffee bar; numerous street cafes and restaurants; a theatre restaurant; restaurants with live jazz; harbour bars; fresh fish grilled over hot coals; fish and chip shops, even an ice cream parlour – all interspersed between wonderful antique and other quaint stores dotted along the coastline. End of the advert for Kalk Bay! Yes, I love living here!

Now, against this backdrop, we go back to the new ex-pizza restaurant, which is on a noisy main road, overlooking very little at all, and away from all the action, which severely limits the ambience. We go back there and assume, because we want to be really kind, that their food and service is great, and we ask 'Why should I eat here?' And quite honestly, I cannot find a good enough reason. Not when I know what else is on offer. Can you find a reason?

So, if I was the restaurant owner and I asked myself the obvious – why, when there are so many established restaurants down the road, with fabulous food and views and loyal clientele, should anyone go out of their way to deal with me in my set-up? – I would not be able to give a good enough answer. There is no support for another deli/pizza/fancy type restaurant in this location. And history bears witness to the fact too. So, we need to look at what *there is* support for and work with that. In other words *allow* the support that exists to support us, and work with it.

What can I offer that nobody else does?

What is there support for in this location? What do the people need? What are they asking for? Start by finding out where you are. Where am I? I am situated opposite one of the most popular and most photographed beaches in Cape Town. What if I offer wonderful takeaway food to the beach-goers? (Which I observe no one else in the area does.) What if I open early so that the regular local early morning swimmers can get a takeaway cup of coffee after their morning swim, and maybe a freshly baked muffin? This way I can build relationships and advertise. What if people can pop in for a quick wholesome lunch in the middle of the day while they are on the beach, or when they take a break from work? (Many of the locals are writers, artists and others who work from home.) What if I have a daily special on offer to eat here or take away? (There is no takeaway food on offer in the area.) What if all the beach-goers could buy their takeaway food and drinks from me?

And in terms of support, we can say that, yes, there is support for *that* venture. Yes, beach-goers would support a place opposite the beach that offered good, reasonably priced food – because everyone needs to eat (and does) on the beach, and no one offers this along the coastline, and people are already buying takeaway food some-where else. Now they can get it hot, and it's one thing less to carry to the beach. Yes, the locals too would support a place that offered a changing range of good take-out food for those nights of no cook-ing, because no one else offers anything like this either, and because there are many creative people living in the area on their own.

And all this can be concluded after simple observation.

Maybe it will happen one day. Maybe I am creating this reality even as I write this. I know a small fortune will be made by anyone who takes on this challenge. Perhaps it will be you. I know that one day someone is bound to see the obvious and act on it. And do you know what's been stopping everyone from doing so? That darned pizza oven.

I hope this case study has helped you to understand that seeing the obvious is almost all you need in terms of finding support for your vision in the real world. Also the acknowledgement that the support is always there, if you but look. And this can most easily be done by asking yourself a few basic and easy questions, and then honestly observing the answers from what is around you.

(PS: As I edit this book some six months later (hooray, *Money Alchemy* is on the shelves!) the ex-pizza parlour is empty once again) . . .

'But why did the first pizza parlour work?'

asks my alert editor Maire. 'Don't you think people will ask that, or want to know something about it?'

I'm not really sure, as it was ten years ago now. I think they had established a solid and faithful client base of regulars, which is vital in these parts. I remember going there and it was a warm and friendly and very Italian pizza parlour. Whatever they had working for them way back then has long been lost, and there does not seem to be any support for what the other owners did between then and now.

We must always keep in the flow of support. Constantly assessing and reassessing what is working and what is not in the present moment. There will be more on this in the section on 'Transforming Leaks and Blocks'. For now, let's get back to our own support and base.

In the following processing you will examine the source of support for your wealth vision and open the channels necessary for creating the support your container requires to make it sturdy. You will also begin the practice of cultivating the ability to observe the obvious. This will help you to see what you need to make all your wishes come true – because the clues are all around you!

It's not about money!

A *very, very* important thing to notice in the above example is that nowhere, in this assessment and in ascertaining support, was the question of money raised. Bear this in mind when you do the following exercise and completely avoid looking at funding, money, overdrafts, investors and fund-raising as a means of support. This is not the support I am talking about. If you think your only means of support or of making a venture happen is raising money, then you need to re-look at the whole venture, from scratch. It's *NEVER* money that supports or creates a venture or a dream. Money is created from a dream. Money is the outcome of a successful venture.

If you are not able to do the processing now, skip to the next section, and come back to this later. But do come back! The successful transformation of your wealth container depends on doing *the processing! Meanwhile, do read through these questions and contemplate them until you return to this section.*

Support for Your Container
Wealth Training Process

Here are some questions you can ask yourself that will help you ensure that your container is properly supported.

> *Before you start, STATE YOUR INTENT! Be clear and specific. For example:*
> > *'It is my intent that this processing will release the flow of wealth in my life and I am able to contain it.'*
> *Keep your pen moving*
> *Write without thinking*
> *Repeat the prompt if you are stuck*
> *Keep it light!*

Write down the answers to the following questions:
1. What will ensure the success of my venture?
2. On what do I base this belief?
3. What support do I need for my dream to be realised?
4. What action will support what I want to do?
5. What connections will support what I want to do?
6. Who will support me?
7. What will support me?
8. What roots do I need to cultivate?
9. What obvious details do I need to see?
10. What other obvious questions do I need to ask?
11. What do I need to observe?
12. What am I not seeing or noticing?
13. What am I missing?

What conclusions can you draw from these observations? Take any decisions you need to and undertake to perform any inspired actions you need to perform.

Execute your actions and decisions.

Exercises to Cultivate the Ability to see The Obvious
Wealth Training Process

1. Really look at your partner today, or someone whom you see on a daily basis, like the bus driver, receptionist, or your boss. What is obvious in their appearance?
2. Look at your hands. Find something you did not notice before.
3. Notice three things on your way to work or to the shops that you did not notice before.
4. Look at your front door. What do you see that you did not see before?
5. Take a different road to work every morning (if possible) for a week. Notice new things.
6. Find three things about your car you did not notice before.
7. What looks different today?

Scrap it and start again

I have gone quite a way along the track of what is actually business advice, and I feel I cannot leave you hanging. I have to answer the obvious: 'What if (in light of the above) I find there is no support for what I have set my heart/mind on doing in the way I wanted to do it?'

'What if my container is not supported?' The best answer I can give you is in the form of clay. Try what you are asking with a piece of clay. Make something without the proper base, watch it collapse, and then try to fix it. It's messy and in most cases, it can't be done. You need to scrap it, and start again.

Sorry, there is no way of getting around this. And it's never too late to do it. Usually it's the huge investment in the ego and the need to 'be right' that keeps us focused on wasting time, effort, and energy in areas that are not yielding results, or in our language, in trying to juggle and balance containers that have no proper support and never had in the first place. If it hasn't worked till now, throwing more time, or energy, or money at it is not going to help.

Stop. Don't waste another day. Step back. Step back. Step back again, and observe. See what is there. See what is not there. See what could be there. Pull your ego out of the computation and put it in charge of figuring out where the support is, and how you can get it.

Remember, there is *always support* : you just need to find it.

All the answers to all the questions you need are all around you. First you need to ask the right questions. Then you must observe. Find the support you need from those around you, from within yourself, from the truth, and from reality. If these support your vision, then your container has a base. Because without support, without a proper foundation, without rooting in reality, without a base, your container will simply topple over.

> *Human affairs are like a chess game:*
> *Only those who do not take it seriously can be called good*
> *players*
> Hung Tzu Ch'eng

Give what you most need to receive

To receive more support, we need to give more support. I don't think I need to elaborate on that.

The following actions will create an energetic support matrix for your wealth vision and your container. Repeat them regularly, particularly when your container seems shaky. Make this a part of your regular wealth creation practice. *Come back to this processing if you cannot do it now. But read through the questions before moving to the next section.*

Cultivating Support
Wealth Training Process

> *Before you start, STATE YOUR INTENT! Be clear and spe-*
> *cific. For example:*
> > *'It is my intent that this processing will release the*
> > *flow of wealth in my life and I am able to contain it.'*
> *Keep your pen moving*
> *Write without thinking*
> *Repeat the prompt if you are stuck*
> *Keep it light!*

1. Whose dream or vision can you support through word or deed today? Do it.
2. Who can you inspire? Do it.
3. How can you help someone get to the next level? Do it.
4. How can you advertise for someone whose work or product you admire? Do it.
5. Take five small pieces of clay the size of your palm.
   Create five identical containers.
   Create five different stable bases for each container.
6. How can you support your own vision?
7. Check all the furniture in your home. If there are any shaky legs on chairs, tables or beds, fix them (properly, not with a piece of paper stuck underneath).
8. Ensure there is nothing in your surroundings that is 'toppling over' because it's not supported.
9. If you routinely wear high heels, ensure they are not so high that you totter around in them looking as if you are about to topple over. Perhaps you need lower heels that support you better.
10. Go back to the container you drew early on. Check the base. If it does not support your container properly, or if it does not exist, correct this. Draw a good, strong, solid base.
11. Put on some good solid music with a good solid earthy beat. While keeping your vision and container in mind, dance and pound your feet into the ground with the intent of grounding and supporting your vision.
12. Who and what are you not allowing to support you?
13. Open your mind to the possibility that there are many ways of doing anything.

Underline or highlight important words and phrases. Summarise into one sentence. List any decisions or inspired action you will take as a result. Execute your decisions and actions. Prepare to receive. Celebrate and rejoice! Acknowledge your transformation with thanks!

Well done! The universe salutes you!

Lie down on the ground (not the bed). Take a few deep, smiling breaths and relax completely. Feel the earth support every part of your body, every muscle and organ and limb. Feel yourself cradled by mother earth. Thank the earth for this support. Know that you are *always* supported. *Always.*

10

The Size of the Container

Is your container big enough to hold your money?

Yes, size does matter

The size of your container will determine how much you can fit into it. Size is closely linked to and should be proportional to the shape of the container. We will be talking further about the container's shape, from the point of view of size, and in relation to other aspects of shape which we have not dealt with yet.

If the container is too shallow, the contents will evaporate. If the shape is too complicated, the contents will not find their way in. (Like those long, complex business plans where you still have no idea what it's all about twenty pages into the document.) If the size is too small, very little can be contained (the 'I just want to pay my bills' syndrome). If it's so big that you cannot contain it, that you cannot find the top, then it will never get full either. The size of the container must be manageable. That means that your dream and goal and vision must be real – to you, that is.

This may seem a contradiction when we have been talking about going for something that seems totally unreal from where we stand at present. Let me explain. The reality lies in the specificity and in the relate-ability and in the ability to have, or in other words to contain, your goal. If you do not know what you want and if you cannot relate to what you want emotionally, in your body and in your mind, then you will be unable to contain it. Your goal must feel real to you, even while it feels scary. It must feel like something you can actually achieve. It cannot be just make-believe fantasy.

It is a very fine line, the line between allowing yourself to enter into and cultivate believing in a 'big, hairy audacious dream' on the one hand, and the dream having actual reality for you in the sense that you can believe it can happen, on the other. The fine line is ability to contain. Do you resonate with what you are saying you want, or is it superficial mumble? Do you feel your gut resonate with what you say you want? Do your words echo throughout your being in truth? Is it really you who is saying this, or is your mind regurgitating your parents, or the media, or a movie you once saw?

If you can't see the edges, it's not a container

More often than not it's a case of our container being too small, but there is definitely a danger in making it so big that you cannot relate to or deal with the sheer enormity of the project. When this happens, it is time for a reality check, a pulling-in of things closer towards you. The size of your container quite literally symbolises the distance between current reality and your wealth vision, because what creates distance is space (and in the 'real' world, time) and the more space in your container, the bigger it will be (and the longer it will take – mostly). If that space becomes so big that you can no longer see where your container begins or ends, you have lost the plot, quite literally.

What this means in real life is a situation where you cannot pay your basic bills, but you create a project which needs two hundred million dollars to get off the ground, and you expect someone to fund it. The gap between current reality and the future is just too big. If the most money you have ever handled or dealt with in your life is a few hundred thousand, two hundred million has the same reality as one hundred and fifty million or three hundred million. It's just not real.

I tell the story in my first book of how I once sat under a tree (just like the Buddha . . . though alas, I did not become enlightened . . . Yet) and listed what I wanted, in a fabric-covered book, at a time in my life when I worked as a consultant for a fund management company, on straight commission. This was in the late eighties, and I lived in a studio apartment with almost no assets, apart from myself, that is. Never forget, *you are the greatest asset you have in life!* So I sat under the tree and wrote my wish list, which included, in addition to a fully paid-up house, a Mercedes sports car and a few other things, 'one million in international currency'.

How was that real to me? Well, don't forget that in the business I ran before that, in the late seventies, hundreds of thousands had gone through my hands. Also, as an investment consultant I was dealing with portfolios worth hundreds of thousands, which later became hundreds of millions. So 'one million', although quite an enormous stretch for my mind at that time, did have reality for me, in a way that ten or twenty million did not, at that time.

You need to increase your container on a gradient. Your money comfort zone needs to graduate from hundreds, to thousands, to tens of thousands, to hundreds of thousands, to millions and so on. This can happen fast, and some of the steps can be skipped out, just as long as it's real.

If you can't see the space between the edges, it's not a container

The equally common problem of creating too small a container was covered in the introduction with reference to the bonsai – a small container will stunt the growth of a tree. The same applies to wealth. Allow enough room for your wealth to expand into. A sense of expansion must occupy every aspect of your life in order for that same expansion to permeate into the area of wealth. Generosity reflects that sense of expansion. So does gratitude.

Generosity does not relate to money alone, it relates to time, it relates to effort, to knowledge, to goodwill, to sharing, to carrying of burdens. Think of the people you know. Are the people who are generous with their money (regardless of how much they have) not also the people who are generous with their time and praise and joy? Are they not also the people who share their energy?

You will find that generous people give much more than just money, and because the more expansive you are the more expansion you will contain, the more generous you are, the more expansion will occur in your life.

> *The best portion of a good man's life – his little, nameless,*
> *unremembered acts of kindness and of love*
> William Wordsworth

Let's look at expansion and generosity for a moment then, and let's look at generosity as something we can expand into. Let's look at it as a skill that we can develop and practise. In the following processes we will reflect on ways in which we can expand our generosity. We will consciously undertake to embrace authentic action that will facilitate this expansion in imperceptible ways.

If you cannot do this processing now, read through the instructions and commit to executing at least one action until you are able to come back and complete the process fully. Please do come back! I'll be waiting.

Expansion and Generosity
Wealth Training Process

Write for two minutes on the following. Allow your pen to write. Think beyond the obvious. Be specific. Be creative. Have fun!

> *Before you start, STATE YOUR INTENT! Be clear and specific. For example:*
> **'It is my intent that this processing will release the flow of wealth in my life and I am able to contain it.'**
> *Keep your pen moving*
> *Write without thinking*

Repeat the prompt if you are stuck
Keep it light!

1. I can expand my wealth through ....
2. I can expand my generosity by ....
3. In my day-to-day life I can afford to give more of my .... List seven things.
4. How I will do this is .... List three ways for each of the seven things mentioned above.
5. I can expand my view of the world through ....
6. I can expand my relationships by ....
7. I can expand myself if ....
8. I will expand my container by ....
9. The key to my expansion is ....

- Underline important words and phrases and summarise into one sentence.
- Draw up a 'to do' list with the three most important things on it.
- Do those things.
- When you are done, pick another three things to do, and do those. Continue until you are finished.

Breathing deeply is a wonderful way to expand, as is spinning round and round with your arms open like children do, which is also very energising. It's also highly therapeutic to fall over on to the ground from dizziness and sheer silliness.

There are obvious acts of generosity like giving of time or possessions to a worthy cause. Do these regularly according to your ability to give at this time.

The less obvious, more difficult, but definitely more transformational options are:

Cultivating Generosity as a Practice
Wealth Training Process

Before you start, STATE YOUR INTENT! Be clear and specific. For example:
'It is my intent that this processing will release the

flow of wealth in my life and I am able to contain it.'
Keep your pen moving
Write without thinking
Repeat the prompt if you are stuck
Keep it light!

1. Take the time to really listen to someone whom you normally avoid because you find them annoying or boring (ouch!). Listen closely and deeply from the heart. Listen as an act of giving. (If you don't know any annoying people (there's always a miss-goody-two-shoes . . .) ask to borrow one from a friend. Make sure to give them back when you're finished.)
2. Open your heart to someone close, and let them know how you really feel.
3. Compliment someone who looks great, especially if you dislike them, and do it from your heart. (Of course you can!)
4. Do something to help someone that scores you absolutely no brownie points, and tell no one. (Try!)
5. Smile at the person next to you in the car, queue, pathway, especially if they are the same sex. Do not do this in a skimpy skirt.
6. Pick up the next tab, especially if it's not your turn.
7. Buy flowers for an acquaintance.
8. Give away something you really love (in South Africa we'd say 'for *sommer*' which means 'just because').
9. Bury the hatchet and call someone you really love, even if it's their fault you're not talking. (Okay, you're allowed to feel just a teensy bit superior . . .)
10. Do that other thing you kept thinking about while you were reading this list. (You know what it is.)
11. Laugh! (Not later – now. Laugh loudly and heartily and from the depths of your tummy.)

- This process should form part of your regular practice. Try to do at least one of these things per week.
- Write about what happened and how it made you feel.

By developing the practice of generosity in this way, your container, and therefore your ability to contain, will expand. When your container expands, more of the wealth which is flowing all around you will be contained. This means you are becoming wealthier, even as we speak.

Well done! Celebrate! And above all else, prepare to receive! And remember to acknowledge your transformation with thanks.

To recap: the size of your container must be something you can relate to, and it must be expansive enough to contain a wealthy you. Cultivating generosity and a sense of expansiveness will ensure you create an expansive container. Weighing the size of your container against your own truth will help you correct any discrepancy in size. The proper balance between give and take will keep your container manageable and balanced. This brings us to the next section, the top of your container.

11

The Top of Your Container

Are you open for wealth to enter?

(Don't) Put a lid on it

The top of your container is where 'things', hopefully wealth, will
enter. Whereas the bottom keeps you grounded in the earth, in
reality, and in the here and now, the top keeps you open to future
possibilities; to expansion; and to the Divine. How open you are
will be in direct proportion to how grounded you are, and to how
strong your parameters are. To put that in money terms means how
much wealth you achieve depends on how much you can keep your
feet on the ground, and how well you can maintain your boundaries. Or, how much money can enter your life depends on how well
you can accommodate or contain it and keep it balanced, without

letting it fizzle away or overwhelm you.

We are looking here at issues of open and closed. And, definitely, if you have a container with a closed top nothing will enter. Closed and open relates to generosity, as well as to the ability to receive, which, as we discussed earlier, is linked to the ability to give. So here at the top we have the culmination of balanced give and take. We have as below, so above and as above, so below.

If you cannot open up the top of your container, you may have the most fabulous shape, the most perfect texture and thickness of walls and the most balanced base ever, but as long as the top is not open, it will never get full. In fact we could argue that without an opening on top, it may not even be a container. If, on the other hand, the opening on top is too big or too wide (which may also be a function of the size being too small, and the walls being too low), everything that enters will evaporate.

The curious thing, though, is that the more 'as below', the more 'as above'. So the more balanced your base is, the more naturally open will be its top.

As below, so above

To open up to wealth, to a magical future, to a wealthy you, is to open up to the unknown. It is to open up to divine intervention, to amazing synchronicities and to miraculous possibilities.

It is also to open up to the truth, to the reality of what you really want and to what you do not want. Truth opens doors for the creation of new realities. Truth opens your heart.

This is risky territory. It is a move into the unknown, the untried, the untested. It is sailing into uncharted shores, which is scary for most of us.

Openness is quite a big subject, and an interesting one. When we think of open people we think of happy, friendly folk who speak their minds and chatter away with everyone they meet. Now although this may be the profile of an open person, it is not automatically the case. Some very extroverted people can have severe boundary issues. You know those friendly people on the plane who insist on chatting to you, and giving you their whole life story, and questioning you about yours, when all you want is to read your book, or to sleep? And they won't take a hint. And you can't get them to stop unless you are downright, absolutely rude. Now, that's not open. That's someone with boundary issues.

On the other extreme, you can have someone who is pretty introverted (the one on the plane reading his book), not very talkative, not over friendly, yet pretty open.

Openness has to do with flow, with allowing, with vulnerability, with taking risk, and with the willingness to move beyond and out of your comfort zone. Openness is basic readiness. It is the readiness to receive, it is the readiness to act, it is the readiness to become, it is the readiness for 'whatever it is, I'm game for it, bring it on!' Openness takes courage, faith and trust, but first of all it takes readiness. Readiness is saying yes.

In Richard Branson's *Screw It, Let's Do It*, he says that he discovered that his staff referred to him as Mr Yes, because more often than not, whatever idea anyone comes up with, he is likely to say yes. Branson believes it is better to say yes to everything and occasionally get something wrong, than to say no to everything and lose many possible opportunities.

So, having harped on about the importance of saying 'no' elsewhere in the book, let's now look at openness and saying 'yes'. This is what is known as a paradox . . . and you will have discovered by now that this book, like life, is full of them!

In the following wealth training you will reflect on your openness and on your ability to say 'yes' in various ways which will culminate in a reflection on the condition of the top of your wealth container. You will then undertake to cultivate more openness through performing various inspired actions and making these a part of your wealth training practice.

If you are unable to do the processing now, read through the questions and reflect on each one quietly to yourself. Come back to doing the exercise in writing later.

Openness and saying Yes
Wealth Training Process

Spend a little time reflecting on your openness and ability to say 'yes' with the help of the following prompts.

Before you start, STATE YOUR INTENT! Be clear and specific. For example:
> *'It is my intent that this processing will release the flow of wealth in my life and I am able to contain it.'*

Keep your pen moving
Write without thinking
Repeat the prompt if you are stuck
Keep it light!

Free write for two minutes on each prompt.
- With people I know I am generally open/not open, because ....
- With people I do not know I am generally open/not open, because ....
- When it comes to new ideas I am ....
- What I am most open to is ....
- What I am least open to is ....
- My automatic response to something new is .... because....... then I ......
- I am very closed to/towards ....
- I always say 'no' to .... Write a list of eight
- I always say 'yes' to .... Write a list of eight
- My heart is ....

- Underline important or significant words and phrases in a different coloured pen. Summarise into one sentence.
- Consider whether your container opening is generally open or closed. Reflect on what this means in your life, whether you would like to change anything, and how you will go about it.
- Act on your decision.
- Record your decisions and intended actions.

> *Openness, patience, receptivity, solitude, is everything*
> Rainer Maria Rilke

Cultivating Openness as a Practice
Wealth Training Process

Here are some ideas that will help to cultivate more openness. Obviously use good sense and discretion, and do not do anything that will expose you to danger.

Before you start, STATE YOUR INTENT! Be clear and specific. For example:
'It is my intent that this processing will release the flow of wealth in my life and I am able to contain it.'
Keep your pen moving
Write without thinking
Repeat the prompt if you are stuck
Keep it light!

- Do a little something you would not normally do, every day for a week.
- Say 'yes' to things you would normally say 'no' to.
- Trust someone you would not normally trust.
- Trust your instincts.
- Give someone the benefit of the doubt.
- Do that thing you have been afraid to do.
- Believe your plan will work and go for it.
- Read the biography of Mother Teresa.
- Drop off your old magazines and toys at your nearest hospital. Pop in and visit the little ones, or anyone else that draws you.
- Stretch out your arms in an open arms gesture and breathe deeply. Do this several times daily.
- Allow your heart to open.

Record any revelations, decisions, or reflections that arise as a result of this wealth training practice.
Go back to the drawing of your container you did some chapters back, and examine the opening. Make any adjustments you need to make.

Through this practice, you are setting up powerful energetic pathways for wealth to flow towards you. Celebrate the fact! Maybe it's time for a party!

I think openness is best summarised in the words of Eileen Caddy who says:

Believe in miracles. Expect the most wonderful things to happen.
Not in the future but right now

Money will not flow towards you if you are closed. Opportunity will not enter if your door is closed. Possibility cannot flourish without the light of day. So draw back the curtains and let the sunshine in.

Open yourself up to wealth, open yourself up to the new, and allow all good things to flow to you. Be open to wealth.

> *Such gardens are not made by singing*
> *'. . . Oh, how beautiful', and sitting in the shade*
> Rudyard Kipling

Amazing Grace

Probably the most significant aspect of the top of your container is the connection with the Divine. When we lose our connection with Spirit, God, Source, we are not open, and we are not in the flow. This connection means different things for different people, depending on your spiritual practice. The key is to have a spiritual practice.

Many of us today have moved away from the religions we were born into. We may no longer feel we fit into the holy houses that our parents worshipped in. However, the Divine dwells in all of us, ready to direct and inspire and guide. Ensure that as a part of your daily life, you find the time to connect with the Divine. There are two aspects of this – talking and listening. Prayer is talking to the Divine. Meditation is listening. Take time to do both, daily. Five or ten minutes is better than trying to do an hour and never managing it.

Perhaps it is nature that inspires you. Perhaps you need to sit under a tree and simply be still, listening. Perhaps a special object inspires you, maybe an icon, or a photo of a teacher; a crystal or a vase of flowers. Use whatever feels comfortable and real for you to start the journey of reconnecting with the Divine.

The benefits and efficacy of both meditation and prayer are well documented and researched. The point is to connect to that which is greater than (though also within) us. That is what will ensure that the top of your container is always properly aligned.

Practise listening to that quiet inner voice. Learn to depend upon, validate and trust your intuition, for it is the voice of God within. Be aware. Look for signs, symbols and omens. Pay attention to your dreams. Observe the mirrors that people hold all around you. Hear the voice of the Divine.

'How do I know it's my intuition?' people always ask me. Just believe.

> *I saw the Lord with the eye of my heart, and I said:*
> *Who art Thou? He said: Thou*
> Al-Hallaj

And remember, whatever you do, let it be light and joyful! Here are the words of Pablo Picasso:

> *God is really only another artist.*
> *He invented the giraffe, the elephant, and the cat.*
> *He has no real style. He just keeps on trying other things*

12

Fullness

Is your container too full for wealth to enter?

In the fullness of time

The last aspect of the wealth container that we will cover is its fullness, although this is more an aspect of the contents than the container itself. Observe, however, whether the container you drew way back at the beginning of this journey was drawn full or empty. At the *Money Well*™ courses, we spend a whole afternoon creating a container out of clay while in a reflective, meditative state. Participants walk around the gardens outside and collect whatever they are drawn to, and use it to decorate their containers. Some people decorate outside or around the container, others fill the inside with flowers or bark, yet others do not decorate at all.

And so the question we are looking at here is: 'Is your container empty or full?' And this takes us to the old story of the student going to the master for guidance. The master offers the student tea. They sit down and the master pours for the student and continues to pour even when the student's cup is overflowing. He says to the student, 'The cup is like your mind, it is full and nothing more can enter, to go further you first need to empty your cup' – or words to that effect. If your container is full, nothing can enter. If it keeps overflowing, it may be time to expand it to a larger one, or empty out some of the contents, or both.

An empty container is like the seeking mind which has space for things to enter. It is like the person ready to receive. It is like the open door before the start of a feast – everything is ready, and the guests are on their way. It is like planted, well tilled, nourished, watered, fertilised land ready to grow plants and bear fruit. So emptiness represents readiness.

Are you ready?

This readiness has many expressions, and it is the culmination of all the preparation that has gone into the creation of the container so far. It is also the most crucial point in the manifestation process – that point of holding a space for what you are manifesting to appear. As you will remember, we have prepared on many levels, all centred around observing what is, deciding on change and aligning intent, feeling, and action to execute that change. We have performed a variety of processes and symbolic acts and put in place new patterns of behaviour to facilitate a new level of beingness.

We have created a specific shape for our container, demarcated parameters and boundaries with our walls. We have processed the material our container is made of, determined an appropriate size, grounded it with the right base and opened ourselves to a wealthy future through an open top. Now we hold the space open.

This means many things. It means we maintain the status quo. It means we ensure parameters continue to be in place, that base, size, material, and top continue to be as we want them. It means that we hold on to our dream. It is the moment just before the manifestation enters consensus reality; it is the point of greatest tension. It is the space of nothing. And in this case literally so, as you have an empty container and you need to keep it that way. Of course nature abhors a vacuum, as we do, and the first thing we try to do is fill it. This desire is often a test of our will and sincerity and determination too.

It was the best of times, it was the worst of times

What happens in real life is something like this. You have done everything in this book like a star. You are now ready, at last, after twenty years of wanting to (or sometimes after a lifetime of wanting to), to start your own accounting business, or restaurant, or gym; or to go off and travel; or to join the circus; or go into the Amazon to photograph piranhas, or to sell up everything to fund a school for orphans.

And here you are, on the eve of your great moment – and let's pause here for a moment to say that even though it's the greatest moment of your life, it is also the very worst; even though you are incredibly excited, you are also filled with dread and fear; even though you are beyond the point of no return, you can just as easily forget the whole unsettling idea and return to life as it was before you picked up that wretched book.

Your mind is throwing all sorts of 'what ifs' at you, as are many of those near and dear. You keep getting emails with the latest statistics on 'Failure Rate for First Time Business Owners' from well-meaning friends. And every time you pick up a newspaper or magazine, there is an article about some failing industry only one step removed from the one you are planning to launch into.

That is the scenario, as you will, or may already have, discovered.

Here you are, on the eve of your great moment, tying up the very last details, and suddenly your boss offers you a rise, or that big account you have been after for five years; or you come into an unexpected inheritance, or you suddenly 'see the light' and realise that going away every weekend may be just as good as travelling abroad for a year; or that photographing local aphids will be just as exciting as the Amazon piranhas; or that it's childish to join the circus, what you should be doing is promoting the best circuses in the world; or that you are not such a great chef anyway, and in fact it's a much better idea to start making muffins and selling them on the train.

Don't ever, ever, 'settle'!

So you're off your mission and on a(nother) mission. You start to promote circuses, bake muffins, go away at weekends, get busy on that new account, and start photographing aphids like crazy. And there you are, you have entered the land of compromise, you have been unable to hold that empty space, so you are filling up your container *with something else.* In other words, you have 'settled'. And ploops, just like that, it's all gone and you are off on a totally different track which, I must hasten to add, is only a good thing a tiny fraction of a per cent of the time.

Don't do it!

Never, ever, ever, give up!
Winston Churchill

All good things come to those who can hold the space

For the first eight months in my new job as telemarketer of a fund management company, many, many moons ago, I earned NOTH-ING. Now I had decided to work mornings only, to earn as much as I wanted (which you can do, when your earnings are commission based), and pursue my other interests the rest of the time. In other words, I wanted to have my cake and eat it, with cherries on top!

I reduced my overheads in preparation, I produced, and affirmed, and rejoiced, but mostly, I *held the space.* Now, everyone near and dear was dumbfounded. They advised and pleaded and begged me to get a 'decent, paying job' which I could have done, quite easily – and based on my background and experience, I could have been earning a huge amount with company car and perks. But I held the space. When need for money became dire, I took on an evening job to cover my overheads, and still *I held the space.* Eight months is a very long time, month by month, comment by comment. But I held the space, I did not settle, and eventually I owned the company that I had telemarketed for!

I always ask folk two questions on my courses, in a variety of ways:
1. What do you want?
2. What will you settle for?

At least 99 per cent of the people are prepared to settle for something other than what they really want. Here's a newsflash: '*You will always get what you're prepared to settle for.*'

Beware of the temptation to go and fill your container with something other than what you really want, at the very last moment, (almost) at the very end of your journey. And forewarned is forearmed, because I can assure you the pull towards some other direction on the eve of your success will always and most assuredly be there.

Long before that happens though, and more relevant to containing money, is the question of whether your container might already be full – because naturally, if it is, nothing else will be able to enter. What can your container be full of, if it's not money? Bullshit, excuses, lies, old dead things, garbage and stuff, and anything you are still holding on to that no longer serves you.

Emptying your cup

Simply put, we need to make space for money to enter our lives. If you do not make space for money to enter your life, where will it go? This question has brought us full circle, back to the need for a container. Making space for money is a symbolic as well as a realistic act.

I remember a friend who for many years wanted to enter into an intimate relationship. Yet her life was full. She ran a business, exercised daily, studied part time, and filled her days and nights with numerous other activities and projects. There was no space for a relationship. There was no time for a relationship. So there was no relationship.

We need to make space. We need to let go of the old to embrace the new. We need to let go of the old belief systems, excuses and feelings about money, self and others. We need to let go of grudges, judgements, and chips on the shoulder, both imagined and real.

We need to let go of the old, dead, smelly, decomposing bodies and garbage rotting away and festering in our container. Yuck!

We need to let go of our current picture of reality: who we are, how we do things, and how we relate to the world. That is what it means to empty your cup. Then we need to enter the place of no-man's-land, that place where we have left the shore, and we have no idea what lies at the other end of the wide open sea. It is the letting-go of all the familiar anchors of our lives. It is not a comfortable place to be, which is why few go there. It is the space of the empty container, waiting to be filled.

When I looked in the mirror, I couldn't recognise my face

I spent eleven years realising my goal to become financially independent so I could teach and write and raise consciousness on the planet unhindered by financial constraints. When I sold my business and moved to Cape Town I left behind everything I knew and loved – my business, clients and staff; my friends; a long-term relationship; my father; my mother who had just passed away; a beloved cat who also passed away; my home; life as I had known it. I had emptied my container and I felt completely lost and bereft.

I remember looking at myself in the mirror and not recognising my face. I remember thinking there is no one here I know, to reflect to me who I am. My container was empty, and so what did I do? Did I hold the space? Did I consider that the new life, the new me, needed time to be created? Alas, no. I panicked, and went straight back into business.

Yes, unfortunately I did not have the benefit of this book . . . So off I went with my ex-business partner and we started an IT recruitment business. I knew how to do business, you see – far more than I thought I knew how to write or teach. Or become the me you see unfolding here as the author of a second book.

Going back into business was easy. I knew how to do that. So we ran and grew that business for three years, before selling it to our staff, who are successfully growing and running it to this day, ten years later.

It's not easy to hold the space open for something new to emerge. The temptation to go back to the known, to the old, is very great, even when you have let go of the old physically.

Your cup runneth over

We will address many aspects of releasing the old quite specifically when we look at transforming blocks and obstacles to money-making in Part II of this book. For the moment, we will deal with emptying our container in a symbolic and general way.

You can empty your container symbolically by emptying out other elements of your life, provided this is done with the proper attention and intention.

Here are some of the classic ways of creating new space in your life, and letting go of things that no longer serve you.

By doing this wealth training, you are making space in your container, and in your life, for more wealth to enter.

If you do not have time to start creating a new wealthy space now, make time. That's how important this is in relation to your container.

> *The beginnings of all things are weak and tender.*
> *We must therefore be clear-sighted in beginnings*
> Michel Eyquem De Montaigne

Creating a New Wealthy Space
Wealth Training Process

It is best to do this wealth training just before, or over a weekend.

Before you start, state your intent; it is preferable to write it down. Something along the lines of *'It is my intent, through the tidying of my cupboards/drawers/car/handbag/garage to let go of the old that no longer serves me and to open up a new space for wealth.'*

Furthermore, as you pull out each item, putting it aside to recycle or give away, reinforce your intent and focus your attention more strongly by reiterating anything relevant or symbolic that may come to mind, accompanied by a mental picture, and some feel-good feelings. Simultaneously, breathe out as you let go of things, and breathe in, filling your tummy and chest as you create new space.

For example:

- 'I let go of what no longer fits' – as you pull out those ill-fitting pants, while breathing out.
- 'I open up the space for new tools' – as you clear a shelf in your garage, while breathing in.
- 'I only keep what makes me feel great in my life' – as you hold on to only your most stunning clothing, and breathe in, imagining a glowing you and feeling what that feels like.

Now, do it!

- Clear out your wardrobes, letting go of what no longer suits you, making space for a new you.
- Clear out your bookshelves, releasing old beliefs, making space for new knowledge.
- Clear out your garage, putting away tools that no longer work, making space for new tools of wealth.
- Clear out the kitchen cupboards, letting go of old food, and cooking utensils, making space for new nourishment.
- Clear out the attic, giving away things you do not use, opening up your flows.
- Clear out the basement, letting go of stored emotions you are sitting on, to create new foundations.
- Clear out your bathroom throwing out old medicine, to make space for a healthier you.
- Clear out your car boot, letting go of things you drag behind you, making your passage to wealth clear and smooth.
- Clear out your desk, opening up the space for order and direction in your life.
- Clear out your handbag, ensuring clarity goes with you wherever you go.

Warning: Do not do this all at once. These seemingly simple wealth clearings, when infused with metaphor and intent, become very powerful symbolic acts which will radically shift both your psyche and your life. Some dust will rise, as dust does during a major spring clean, so be ready for that too. You may find yourself needing to take a reduced schedule for a day or two, you may even develop a cold, or diarrhoea. You may feel down or angry, or irritable. This is your body's way of letting go of the old. Allow it to pass. You will feel a new sense of purpose and clarity later, and you should feel a whole lot of energy too.

This wealth training will create clarity, purpose, and a new sense of space in your life and in your wealth programme. Repeat it regularly, at the turn of every season, to continue the enormous benefit that it can yield. But now, have a piece of chocolate cake and a cappuccino (especially if you've been detoxing . . .) – you deserve it! Well done!

I can see clearly now . . .

Keeping your container clear is very important for the creation of wealth and for your advancement in life. You will not find many highly successful people working or functioning in disorder and chaos. It is just not possible. Even if they themselves are not the tidy sort, they will have a highly organised secretary. It's just the way it is, and it goes with the territory.

Let's face it, if you cannot organise your drawers, how will you organise a whole restaurant, or an accounting company with branches nationwide? Do you know how? You will do it exactly as you do your drawers. Because how you do anything is how you do everything, and because everything is connected.

The good news is that you can prepare, and cultivate, and become really great at what you do with those drawers, which will take far less effort, time, energy, and capital than starting a company, so that when you *do* get into that business, it will be as easy as pie!

In the next chapter we will recap everything we have covered about containment and the container, with specific regard to money, and with a relevant reflection on each point.

Finally, you will find solutions to common money ailments and a quick wealth – trouble-shooting guide which will solve all your money problems! Poof! Just like that!

13

The Money Well™ Summary

Solutions to Common Money Ailments and Wealth Trouble-shooting Guide

The Wealth Container Summary

- There *must be* A CONTAINER

  To contain your wealth and vision
  What do you want?

- It must have a specific SHAPE

  Your specific goal, destination new beingness. The way you want it to make you feel
  How does it look and feel?

- Must be made of flexible expandable MATERIAL

  Held together by your intent, will and feelings
  How much do you want it?

- Must have firm clear WALLS

  The choice of what is in and what is out
  Your boundaries and parameters
  What will you do to get it?
  What do you refuse to do to get it?

• Be of an appropriate SIZE	Able to relate to having the goal Able to expand enough to have it *Where will you put it? Does it fit? Can you fit into it?*
• Have a solid, balanced BASE	Goal is grounded in reality *What must you do to create it? What is obvious?*
• Be open on TOP	Be open to receive Keep container clear and empty, free of garbage and clutter *What must you let go of to get it?*

Solutions to Common Money Ailments

Quick remedies for common ailments on the road to wealth expansion

Below are some common challenges you may encounter on your wealth journey. Contemplate the questions offered in response, and read the appropriate section recommended, making sure you complete any processing in that section.

• I don't know what I want

FULLNESS	Read Fullness	Empty your container
SHAPE	Read Shape	Get specific

What do I need to let go of in my life that is weighing me down?

• I want so much, where do I start?

WALLS	Read Walls	Clarify your parameters – what will you have inside and outside your container

If I could be, do, or have only one thing before I die, what would that thing be?

• How do I know what I want will be good for me? *And/Or*

How can I ensure my wealth creation will not harm others and the world?

| TOP | Read Top | Open to guidance and trust |
| WALLS | Read Walls | Clarify your boundaries |

How can I open to trusting myself and the world around me?

- No matter what I do, I stay in the same place, wealth-wise

| FULLNESS | Read Fullness | Empty your container |
| SIZE | Read Size | Expand your container |

How can I expand my life and self to contain more?

- I have wonderful ideas and talents, but no funding to make them happen.

SIZE	Read Size	Expand your container
BASE	Read Base	Ground your vision in reality – act!
MATERIAL	Read Material	Fortify your will and intent

How committed am I to this vision? What action/s can I perform to make it happen?

- I always get to a certain point in my wealth programme, and then everything falls apart

BASE	Read Base	Firm up your foundations
WALLS	Read Walls	Tighten your parameters
MATERIAL	Read Material	Pull together your will and intent

What pattern is being repeated, and how can I change it to a pattern that serves my intent?

- How do I get to make money, when I need money to get started and I don't have it?

| TOP | Read Top | Open yourself up to receive |

BASE	Read Base	Create an action plan and act
SHAPE	Read Shape	Get specific

What would I be doing if I knew the money was on its way?

- I am comfortable; how do I move from this to very wealthy?

SHAPE	Read Shape	Create a new container
SIZE	Read Size	Expand your ability to have
		Connect with a feel-good feeing

How can I expand my life and self to contain more?

- How can I control the many unknown factors out there that could cause my vision to fail?

WALLS	Read Walls	Choose what you want in and out your container
TOP	Read Top	Open yourself to trust
MATERIAL	Read Material	Cultivate your intent and feel-good factor

How can I incorporate more fun and joy in my life?

- How do I know I really want to be wealthy?

I have been rich and I have been poor, rich is better
Marlene Dietrich

The Money Well™ Wealth Trouble-shooting Guide

Here are the various aspects of a container with the most common problems relating to each aspect. It is important to bear in mind that everything is connected, and nothing is absolute. There is normally a range of causes behind any symptom. This is a simplified checklist, covering the most obvious and common aspects for each element of a container. You will find considerable overlap. Don't panic, become wealthy!

- SHAPE

  Challenges relate to:

  Keyword: Specificity

  Inability to get started

  Not knowing what you want, where to go next, what to do next

  All issues around knowing versus not knowing

  All issues related to confusion and vagueness

- MATERIAL

  Challenges relate to:

  Keyword: Durability

  Inability to keep going, complete, or keep focus

  Inability to keep positive, fear of unknown

  All issues relating to things falling apart, or not lasting

  All issues relating to being let down, and failure to deliver

- WALLS

  Challenges relate to:

  Keywords: Boundaries and Parameters

  Ability to contain money created

  Expenses continually cancel out gains

  All unforeseen calamities, or getting what you don't want

  All issues relating to compromise, and not getting what you do want

- BASE

  Challenges relate to:

  Keywords: Grounding and Action

  Inability to take vision into reality

  Lack of support from people, situations, things, self

  All issues relating to things falling apart, or not bearing fruit

  All issues relating to action versus inaction and waiting for 'something' before you can start

- SIZE
  Challenges relate to:

  Keywords: Ability to Have
  Inability to relate to or believe in
  vision or goal
  Inability to go to next level
  All issues around problems with
  movement and stop-start action
  All issues around inability to
  maintain gains

- TOP
  Challenges relate to:

  Keyword: Openness
  Confusion around purpose and
  the wealth creation journey
  All issues related to judgement
  given or received; and deserving
  All issues around trust of self and
  others
  All issues around open versus
  closed

- FULLNESS
  Challenges relate to:

  Keyword: Receptivity
  Inability to receive and give
  Wealth, things, people seem to
  be taken away
  All aspects relating to the
  creation of space, and waiting
  All aspects relating to being full,
  closed, and holding on to

In closing (or should that be opening?)

I would be not only surprised, but absolutely shocked, if by now (having done all the relevant processing and reflections like a star), you have not already seen quite visible, clear, unmistakable progress, signs, wonders and even a marked increase in your wealth profile. You have probably entered a completely new space with regard to your view of wealth, yourself, and your vision. You have reshuffled your psyche completely. You have let go of all sorts of old beliefs, feelings, and luggage that no longer serve you. You have done fabulously well!

WELL DONE! Congratulate yourself. Allow time to absorb. Luxuriate in your achievement. Go out for a fabulous meal, or prepare one at home. Celebrate! Lightly reflect on how far you have come in such a short time. In about a week's time, list all the changes and shifts you have undergone. For now, relax and absorb and celebrate. Take time out to say to yourself:

WOW, YOU ARE REALLY ON A WEALTH EXPANSION JOURNEY! WHAT A STAR!

No, don't be modest, someone's got to do it. And who knows better how fabulous you truly are than you? Let's face it, that's the truth of the matter.

> *The alchemists knew the necessity of creating the inviolate vessel*
> *and giving the elixir all the time it needed to transform into*
> *gold*
> Deena Metzger

Oh, and before I forget, here's how the story ends . . .

Drinking deeply from the Well
Finishing a tale

One day, tired and disillusioned, the young girl left the village and ran into the forest. She ran deep, deep inside the forest where she had been told never to go. And as she wandered further and further within the forest's heart, the light began to change. A golden glow was emerging in the distance, and when the young girl found its source, she saw a well.

But this well was unlike any well she had ever seen before. This well radiated light and a faint scent she could not place except that it made her feel joyful and content all at once.

'Come, drink,' said the well. And the young girl did. And as she drank she remembered her dream of so long ago. She remembered stepping out of the limousine in her golden dress and her tiara and nodding to all the people. She remembered the feeling of being rich and famous and she stood up, smiling, her head held high, and she walked once again swaying her bountiful hips, and nodding to her imaginary audience. Round and round the well she walked, shaking hands, waving, accepting flowers and signing autographs. She was a famous movie star, she remembered!

'*Yes, yes,*' said the well.

For seven days and seven nights the young girl drank deep of the well, and she remembered. She remembered who she was and where the path lay before her. And at the end of the seventh day she emerged from the forest, with a spring in her step, and a light shining in her eyes. She was a movie star! She knew this now. And as she passed through the villages on her way home, others too knew who she was. They were not fooled by her bare feet or her homespun dress, for she held herself like a queen and she radiated the essence of 'superstar'.

Soon many people had gathered around her, touching her, shaking her hand, asking for her autograph. And when she finally arrived at her village, she was not at all surprised to find her bewildered mother standing next to a long silver limousine.

'Look, my daughter, they have come for you,' her mother said. 'Just like you said they would, when you were a little girl. Do you remember, my daughter? Do you remember?'

'Yes, mother,' the daughter replied. 'Now I remember everything!'

And do you suppose that the young girl went on to become a famous movie star?

Of course she did!

The End, and a New Beginning

Part II

How to Clear Obstacles to Wealth

Transforming Leaks and Blocks to Wealth Flow and Wealth
Containment

*What can obstruct the flow of money? What can block the flow
of life?*

1

The Flow

How do you flow through life? How does your wealth flow?

Reflections on Flow

1
The flow of money is the flow of energy
Energy is all around us, unseen
Money is all around us unseen

2
All rivers flow towards the sea
Water is both the river's source and destination
The river leads the water to the sea
The river contains the water's journey

Without a river, the water cannot get to the sea

3

Money will flow towards its source and destination
You are the money's source and destination
Wealth flows along an unseen river to your container

4

Money flow runs on a river of energy
Money flow is contained by your energy flow
Money flow is contained by your own clear flows

5

Energy flow is how you move through the world
Energy flow is how you communicate in the world
Energy flow is how you connect with the world
Your energy flow creates an unseen river

6

Wealth flows along your unseen river
The wealth river is under the ground
The wealth river is hidden in the dark
The wealth river is your shadow waiting to transform

7

Wealth flows along your unseen river
Life flows along your unseen river
You flow along your unseen river
You are the flow and the river

8

The wealth river leads money to its destination
The wealth river directs the flow of money
The wealth river contains money's journey

9

You are the river, the journey, and the destination
You are the wealth flow

The flow

Directing the flow of money, or to put that more accurately, allowing the flow of money into our life and container, is most easily represented by my second law of moneymaking which is 'Clean Flows'. What this means quite simply is that for the flow of money, which is the flow of energy, to reach your container you need a river or pipe for it to flow through. You also need to keep that river or pipe clear and unobstructed, and you need to keep the flow clean and clear too. For if you do not have a river or pipe for money to flow through, or if that piping becomes clogged, or that river becomes obstructed, then, even with the most desirable container, it will be difficult for the flow of money to reach you.

A river runs through it

So here we will look at flow. Energy flow, communication flow, your flow through life, and what obstructs that flow, and ultimately the flow of money through your life. We will also look at the condition of your piping or river in relation to your life and money.

We are looking at how this container that we have been so painstakingly constructing and refining will become filled with money. Of course the sceptics will say, hard work, obviously, how else will money come? But we know that hard work alone is not enough. For if it was, would you be reading this book? So, we are taking our metaphor of container and viewing it not only as our wealth goal and destination and potential of a new beingness, but also as the recipient of something that flows, like water, or energy, or money. And as such, as well as for the purpose of discussing flow more fully, we are viewing container as a dam or perhaps even the sea. We are looking at money as something that is flowing, like water along a river or pipe towards this container which is a dam or sea.

How do you flow through life, and how does your life flow? Do you flow like a dancer? Gracefully, beautifully, moving in time to the rhythm of life? Do you march, in military precision, looking straight ahead, ignoring everything else along the way? Do you dart and duck and dive, avoiding attack, running through life under cover? Do you strut through life, brandishing a flaming sword, cutting down the opposition along the way? Or are you carried, reclining on the back of an elephant, sipping cocktails, draped in veils, as pages herald your arrival with flutes, and scatter rose petals? (Yes, the last is my favourite means of travel too.)

Go with the flow

The art of surrender, of flow, of graceful acceptance, of allowing what is to unfold, or in other words, of being in the moment, may seem at odds with the intentional creation of a future, but it is not. It can be looked at like this. With choice, focus, attention and intent, you choose your dance. You decide if you wish to do the salsa or the tango. You select your partner, and your costume. You learn your steps and you practise them until you can move smoothly, effortlessly, with perfect timing. (This will involve some discomfort – getting fit and into shape, letting go of habits that do not serve the dance, replacing drinking practice with dancing practice and so on.) Then, when it is time to dance, you abandon yourself to the music. You allow yourself to enter the moment totally, and let the music take you where you are both going. That is flow. You may have never heard a song before the moment of the dance, but you are fit, you are practised, and you know the steps – so no matter what music plays, you can flow with it, gracefully and elegantly.

You cannot change the music in the middle of a dance. You can only move with it. The music will continue to flow. If you resist it, it will flow anyway. If you try to dance to another rhythm you will only fall out of step. Such is the nature of flow.

Spend a moment considering the flow of those around you. Consider how they actually move. Is it fast or slow? Are they in a rush or always late? Are they always on time? Do they barge in or get left out? Do they stop, start, stop, start, everything they do? Do they run from one thing to another? Do they dance?

See the correlation between how they flow and how money appears to flow in their life. Do this without judgement (okay, maybe just a little, and only if you have something to smirk about). Reflect and observe, bearing in mind this is only your viewpoint and your perception, and not absolute reality. Now reflect on flow in your own life, using the exercises below. *If you cannot do this now,* move on to the next section, but do come back!

Travellers, there is no path, paths are made by walking
Antonio Machado

Looking at Life Flow
Wealth Training Process

Write without thinking using the prompts below. Allow your pen to write for the recommended time. If you become stuck, repeat the prompt. Do not censor your writing. Allow yourself to be surprised by new discoveries.

Write for two minutes on each prompt
- My flow through life is ....
- The way I move is ....
- The way I flow is ....
- The pattern of my flow is ....
- What speeds up my flow is ....
- What slows down my flow is ....
- What stops my flow is ....

Write for a few seconds on each of these prompts
- The colour of my flow is ....
- The dance of my flow is ....
- The fragrance of my flow is ....
- The music of my flow is ....
- The emotion underpinning my flow is ....
- The shape of my flow is ....

Write for two minutes on each prompt
- I flow better when ....
- My flow is like ....
- I dislike people who flow like ....
- I like people who flow like ....
- I can improve my flow through ....
- My timing is ....
- I am always .... late/early/on time because ....

143

Review what you have written and underline important words and phrases in a different coloured pen. Summarise in a sentence. Write down any decisions you want to make, and any inspired action you want to execute as a result of your realisations.

Put your attention on flow. Observe yourself flowing through your life, without judgement, simply observe yourself and choose to make any changes you think are necessary.

Freeing the body inevitably leads to freeing the heart
Gabrielle Roth

How do you go with the flow?

The way money flows will reflect the way other areas of your life flow. In particular the state of your plumbing, both in the bathroom and in your body, can be a very significant indicator of this. Plumbing helps to direct and regulate the inflow and outflow in your house or body. Examine the plumbing in your house. Are your pipes constantly blocked? Do your taps leak? Does water trickle in, instead of flowing consistently? Does your sewage overflow? Examine the symbols in your life from a higher perspective. Allow your own personal meaning to emerge.

Examine your own eliminatory system. Are you constipated, or do you suffer from diarrhoea as an ongoing pattern and condition? Do you eat enough, or are you overeating? Are you overtaxing your system and becoming congested?

Now this may seem a strange line of questioning to find in a money book, but the truth of the matter is that . . . yes, you've guessed it, everything is connected! Of course common sense must prevail, and sometimes stuff does just happen. It is always best to start by fixing whatever needs fixing, before going into deep contemplation. We are looking for patterns here, not isolated events. Because, yes, at some point the geyser will go and, yes, at some point we all get diarrhoea. However, if there is an ongoing pattern, usually stretching over time, then there may be something there to look at.

Dripping taps and leaking anything is symbolic of money seeping away. Water is traditionally symbolic of emotion too, so there is also that link, which we will not go into too deeply in this book. However, be aware that dripping and leaking (and also exploding things) signify excess emotion that may need to be released in a more conducive way.

Growth will happen, with or without you

Let me pause here for a moment to say something important. One way or another we will grow in this life. We will go through all the lessons we are here to learn, however our belief system packages the concept of lessons. Whether we believe in heaven, or karma, or destiny, or actualisation of self, we will grow, and we will change, and whether it is for better or for worse is up to us. It is also up to us to choose our playing field. I believe that we can choose our dance in this life, because that is what free will is all about, *once you are conscious enough to exercise it.* This is a key point. You can consciously choose to learn your lessons according to and within your own parameters.

In other words, you can decide, and then tell yourself, that you want to do your processing and growing within the confines of meditation, or therapy, or internally with conscious awareness, rather than work out your issues in the physical world around you. Once you have made this choice, with intention and attention, over time, you will find that there is less and less happening 'out there', as it will all be happening inside of you. It's actually always happening inside of us, we just don't always notice.

You will need to remind yourself of this choice repeatedly, till it becomes your new pattern. You need to bear in mind also that you will be unable to control everything; after all, you are not God. When you take ownership of your issues and growth in this way, though, you will find that while life externally becomes a lot more manageable and smooth, facing yourself can become quite a challenge. I will tell you what happened to me.

I finally put it all together, and then I lost where I'd put it

When I sold my portfolio management business some seven years ago (ten, at time of final edit), I retired and moved from Johannesburg to Cape Town. So here I was, having realised and achieved pretty much all my major life goals and targets. I was thirty-nine years old, wealthy, debt free, living in a stunning house overlooking the sea, with a gorgeous man soon to be my husband, free to do anything I pleased with my time – life doesn't get any better than this. So guess what happened? While my physical world continued to glow spectacularly like the best of Hollywood movies – everything was working, nothing broken down – I fell apart.

Yes, it was definitely burnout after so many years of stress and overwork and, yes, it was due to too much change too suddenly in my life and, yes, I was suffering from post-traumatic stress syndrome after a hijacking experience; yes, all of that was true. But it was also a time of enormous transformation. You see, I had this dream of becoming a teacher and healer and writer, once financial success was achieved. And in my innocence, I imagined that I could simply step from one life into another. I thought I would just exchange my business suit and perfectionism and attitude and speed and stress, for a flowing skirt, smiling tranquillity, relaxed measured steps and compassion. Well, was I naive or what?

The powers that be said, okay, if that's what you really want to do, let's get started. Let's get you ready. Let's get you transformed from this one extreme to the other. And as I now had all the time and all the space for some really major transformation, on it came. You know how people look at you strangely, when you try to answer a simple 'how are you?' with anything other than 'brilliant' when your life looks like a picture book? The strange-look response is also something that is a challenge for you, yourself. Because part of you is saying, 'For heaven's sake, why are you not deliriously happy? What's wrong with you? Why are you falling apart now?'

But this is how transformation will take place in our lives if we choose (with focused intent) to keep it separate from our material success and well-being. We will simply fall apart, or release angst, pain and suffering for seemingly *no apparent reason*, and without any trigger or input from the world around us.

That is what you have to contend with if you choose to work out your transformation internally, away from the physicality around you, or you can stay with the faulty plumbing. The choice is yours (mostly). I really do choose and prefer to work out my stuff in the privacy of my own home, no matter how bizarre my mind finds this. I have found that I can experience anguish and distress and pain and anxiety and major suffering without ever leaving my armchair, while everything continues to move smoothly around me! How cool is that? (This is called black humour.)

Let's get back to plumbing. We have introduced the idea that you can choose not to have your plumbing involved in your transformation process. We will process more fully around blocks and leaks in the section on obstacles. For now, simply put your awareness on plumbing, both interior and exterior, and observe without judgement whether there are any recurring patterns in either or both. In particular, reflect on plumbing in relation to the general flow in your life.

You have by now begun to see the connections and patterns between money flow and other types of flow in your life quite clearly. So with that in mind, let us look at money flow itself. *If you cannot do this exercise now, do come back to it later! Simply reading this book will be nowhere near as effective as doing the processing!*

> *I am an old man and have known a great many troubles,*
> *but most of them never happened*
> Mark Twain

Looking at Money Flow
Wealth Training Process

Write without thinking, using the prompts below. Allow your pen to write for the recommended time. If you become stuck, repeat the prompt. Do not censor your writing. Allow what emerges to emerge.

Write for two minutes on each prompt
- My money flows through life like ....
- The pattern of my money flow is ....
- What speeds up my money flow is ....
- What slows down my money flow is ....
- My money flow becomes blocked or stuck by ....
- My money flow stops when ....
- Money flows better when ....

- I can improve my money flow through ....

Write for a few seconds on each of these prompts
- The colour of my money flow is ....
- The number of my money flow is ....
- The fragrance of my money flow is ....
- The taste of my money flow is ....
- The emotion underpinning my money flow is ....
- The shape of my money flow is ....

Review what you have written and underline important words and phrases in a different coloured pen. Summarise in a sentence. Write down any decisions you want to make, and any actions you want to execute as a result of your realisations.

Flow in general can be enhanced through dancing, swimming, swirling (like the dervishes, or young kids); wearing hair loose (especially if it is usually tied up tightly), wearing less constricting clothing (especially flowing skirts for the ladies); breath work and general movement, especially if you are normally sedentary. Of course attention and intention has to be directed towards these rather ordinary changes, transforming them into symbolic acts of transformation.

The flow cycle, like any other cycle, can be broken up into three parts – beginning, middle, and end. No matter what you are doing there is the point at which you start, or the beginning, then the middle part is when you are actually doing the thing, and the end is when you finish. It sounds quite simple, and it is. Moreover, it is a most useful tool in diagnosing where you become stuck in life, in doing things, and in moneymaking.

Using the basic 'start, continue, stop' model of a cycle, you realise that there are only three parts to anything you do. There are only three phases that you have to deal with. Whether it's piano practice or starting a business, or tidying up your desk, you are, at any moment in time, in one of those three phases. How you become stuck becomes a matter of where you become stuck, and is therefore easy to remedy and thus continue the flow. Because flow is nothing more than a continuous and smooth series of cycles.

All journeys start with that first step

Getting stuck at the beginning part of a cycle is having problems with getting started. This is when we talk and talk but never get to doing. Or we continuously make starting conditional on something else, so we think we have to do this thing and that thing before we can start, and we delay and delay, and never get around to starting.

In piano practice it looks like this. I want to resume my piano playing and have set aside two hours for this while the kids are at pottery class. But before I start, I think I need first to tidy up the room, and then I discover all these photos in a pile which I have been meaning to put into the album and so I 'quickly' do that, and then I do a few other things totally unrelated to piano practice 'quickly' too, by which time there is only half an hour left, and so I naturally decide that there's not enough time, so I will leave the practice till tomorrow, when I get into a whole new range of unrelated activities. And if I do this for a few days, I eventually forget all about the fact that I was intending to resume my piano playing, as I am now completely misdirected and busy spring-cleaning the whole house or reshuffling photo albums.

In business it looks something like this. I have this really great idea that I can sell little stools to people outside sports games at the weekends. I tell everyone about it, and they all agree it's a fabulous idea. I know where to buy the stools wholesale, and I can buy a few thousand with my savings, but I think I will probably need many, many more stools than that. I don't know how many stools I will need, and I think I should do market research, and that I need a business plan, and a strategy, and a bank loan, before I can start. So I spend my savings on market research and a business plan and strategy. And the market research reveals that purple plastic stools are what is needed, which is a problem because the ones I can get wholesale are khaki canvas, and the business plan covers supplying the whole nation with stools imported from China (they are much cheaper in bulk there), at a cost of ninety-seven million, which the bank will never extend to me as I have no collateral. So I mope around, telling everyone I had this great idea, but I couldn't finance it, 'because you need money to make money' and so on, with which everyone naturally agrees, and I vaguely resolve to try to find an investor to finance my plan, which I have actually given up on, but one has to maintain face.

Then I see an Indian, or Greek, or Nigerian vendor selling the selfsame khaki canvas stools outside the soccer game, and for twice the price that I had planned to sell them. And the stools are selling like hot cakes! And I kick myself. Twice. And I deserve to.

That is failure to start. And it is very, very, common. While coaching and teaching the *Money Alchemy* courses I came across many people with truly fabulous ideas who simply needed to just do it! I am happy to report that many of them have since actually done just that.

If you want to practise the piano, practise the piano. If you want to sell stools, sell stools. If you want to run workshops, run workshops. If you want to write a book, write a book. Unless you require training for what you plan to do, like becoming a doctor perhaps, in which case, do the training. Yes, I know there are businesses which require capital, and that is what banks are for. The key is to start. The secret is to do. Put as little as possible between you and the start line. Do not delay. Do not get hung up. Start.

You will never make or contain money until you start making or containing it. And that requires a decision. A plan or idea needs to go from fantasy into the realms of a decision to execute. Until that point, you have not started. It's like a journey. You can say I want to go away, I need a holiday, I like Spain, but until you decide to go to Spain during the summer holidays, you have not started. Once you have started, the path is set. Once you have decided to go to Spain, you do not need someone to tell you why it's a good idea to go there. You do not need someone to tell you that it may be more beneficial to go to France, or that you may not make it to Spain because their grand-aunt did not.

BEGIN IT NOW! DO IT!

What do you need to do to get started? Nothing! Just start!

Today isn't any other day, you know
Lewis Carroll

Keeping it flowing

Once you have started, you need to keep going. That's the *continue* part of a cycle. Many people stop at *start*. They open the business doors, or the money flow, and leave it at that. Business does not run itself, even if you have staff; money does not flow itself, you need to keep going. Whereas starting is a decision, continuing is a matter of attention – keeping your eye on the ball, as they say. You have to keep doing. It is also a matter of perseverance. I remember reading once that the difference between a good salesperson and a great salesperson was simple repetition, or the number of times you were prepared to do it again. And, definitely, this is true. When you have already had a full day, can you go for just one more sale, and then another? That's what differentiates the good from the great.

To keep going requires stamina and determination. It also requires vision, which is that container again, and I am sure you are seeing the connections between what we are looking at here and what we have discussed before. To keep flowing, to keep going, not to stagnate – it is really simply a matter of attention. Looking to see what's there, what is happening, what is not happening, what should be happening, making the changes, cycles within cycles, one after the other, perfecting and optimising the flow.

If you keep starting things and not carrying through, if you go from one moneymaking venture to the next and stop because at some point (usually the same point) something goes wrong, if your flow seems to be start-stop, start-stop, then you need to look at *continuing* your flow.

There are many reasons that flow becomes blocked, and we will look at those now. We are working with the metaphor of money as a flow of energy, as something liquid and in motion, flowing down some piping towards the containment of a dam, which we are creating.

The flow of money, being energy, is endless, without beginning or end, immeasurable, certainly plentiful and abundant. How much reaches you, however, depends on how wide your piping is, and of course, how much you can contain beyond that depends on the size of your container, as we discussed before.

Imagine a torrent of water, energy, money, rushing towards you from the top of a great thundering waterfall. It falls down in vast quantities, travels along a broad river until it disappears into an underground tunnel, a pipe, *your* pipe leading to *your* wealth container. If the pipe leaks or is too narrow or becomes blocked, the money will never reach you. And the tricky part is that the piping is under the ground. Like the night, like the shadows, like regular plumbing, it cannot be seen with the naked eye, yet we must ensure its proper functioning.

How do we know piping is blocked or leaking? Though we may not be able to actually see the piping itself, the evidence of its malfunctioning will be there, pretty much like regular plumbing. There are many reasons why our flow in life becomes blocked, or leaks or stagnates, why our money comes in fits and starts.

The most common obstacles to moneymaking are **belief systems, relationships, unfinished business, attitude and unsuccessful actions.**

Transforming obstacles is the most significant part of any journey, because not only does it clear our path to wealth, not only does it create flow and ease in our lives, it also enables us to grow and expand as beings. The transformation is a transmutation of our dark, shadowy, underground, unseen parts into pure gold. And when we can uncover the gold within, we will uncover the gold without. That is natural law.

You are not finished till you finish

The final part of any cycle is the *stop* part, or the end. This may seem quite obvious, but it is not. Bringing a cycle to its conclusion, finishing something off properly, wrapping it all up, is probably the most crucial point of anything we do, yet we usually do not even see this part of the cycle as existing. How you end something is often far more important than how you started or continued it. And unless you know how to end it, nothing will happen. Ending it means doing that last five or ten per cent, which usually takes ten times more energy and effort than the preceding ninety to ninety-five. It means holding the space for things to unfold right till the very, very end. It means breaking through the ceiling of the known, going beyond the barriers of the 'can do', and giving away your comfort zone for good.

That is what needs to happen to finish, to get to the end. And once you have come to the end, you need to go through the finish line. Like an athlete who runs and runs in a race, you need to find and give that last spurt of energy and then go through that finish line. It's no use stopping just before you cross the line to have a smoke break, because *you are not finished.* The ending is what opens the doors to new beginnings, continuing the flow.

So many people drop the ball at the very end. They give up, or are unwilling to go that extra mile to ensure they finish. There are many expressions of this phenomenon, and most are not directly related to the subject of money acquisition itself. Yet this simple little detail will make or break your ability to contain wealth. If you cannot finish, your money quest will never end, so you will never realise your goal. It's quite simple really.

Dropping the ball is not just a physical non-doing, it's mostly psychological. Because if you don't drop it in your mind, you've not dropped the ball. It's the psychic tension that we have been training our will to tolerate that is key.

To finish, you must cross the finish line

Crossing the finish line also means taking home the spoils. Once the container is full you need to use the contents, enjoy the wealth, acknowledge it's there, and take it home. Finish the cycle. *And give thanks.*

Let's look at some examples. In a general sense we are looking at how we finish off things and, in particular, things we are walking away from. Like the end of a job, or a project, or a relationship. Do we end them well, with pride and dignity and grace? Do we finish things off beautifully or are we simply sloppy? Do we say, 'well it's no longer my job, let the next person deal with it'? This is a matter of personal pride; it has nothing to do with the circumstances surrounding the ending of whatever it is. Do we resolve the end of things, or do we let them hang, unfinished in the ether? What is important is not whose fault it is, only how *we* finish.

I sometimes ask participants to bring in various documents providing details regarding their business to the Business Alchemy course. The difference between finishing and not finishing is the difference between bringing in the few pages of documents, and bringing the documents in a plastic-covered folder with the company name and logo on the front. There is no doubt about who is finishing here.

Finishing also relates to closing the sale. How many times have you tried to buy something, where the sales person cannot get it, and keeps trying to sell you the thing you have already decided not to buy? They don't know when to stop, and just take the money.

Naturally this ties back to asking, which we covered earlier on, because closing the sale requires getting to the point of saying 'that will be three thousand dollars, please', and many people will do *anything* but ask for that payment, especially if they themselves are taking the money home.

In a business, it means investing in a till. I remember going to consult in a retail store and I could not find a place to pay. An old petty cash tin was eventually produced. This is not finishing. Nor is it finishing when people look at you strangely when they need to give you change for a one hundred note because they don't have it in their petty cash tin, as if this is some huge breach of etiquette on your part. This is a definite lack of proper finishing. As it is when you need to chase someone to invoice you after a job is done, and then you need to call them again for their bank details. It is all simply not finishing properly. It's not taking the money. Not being ready to receive. At the end of the wealth cycle, you need to take the money.

Every ending is the seed of a new beginning, so as you close a door remember that it also marks the opening of the next door. End a cycle as you would like to start the next one. See the ending as the foundation of a new beginning – end beautifully, gracefully, smoothly, with no loose ends. And remember always to give gratitude and thanks. Although the exchange of an article or service for money which is received, may be (and is) the proper end of a cycle, the attitude of gratitude and the giving of thanks (which is not needed, but is in effect the equivalent of putting that 'little bit of extra' in) is what will determine not only a superior finish, but will pave the way for a truly fabulous new start.

So put your attention on finishing off things, ending cycles, bringing things to a close, going that extra mile to get it done, and receiving what is due to you at the end of a cycle with gratitude and thanks. We will process around finishing cycles in the section on unfinished business.

Here is one of my personal favourite maxims: *The end is the only thing that is left to remember.* And it's quite a thought.

> *Every exit is an entry to somewhere else*
> Tom Stoppard

Putting it all together

We have been looking at flow as a stream of ever-moving energy that we are a part of, and we have looked at how we flow in life, and how life and money flow through us. We have likened money flow to a river of water flowing along an underground pipe towards the dam which is our wealth container. We have said that flow is a cycle which has a beginning, a middle, and an end. We have looked at failure to get going or start a cycle, the problem of continuing the flow, and inability to bring the cycle to a close. All these aspects present as obstacles to money flow, or blocks and leaks in the underground piping that carries our money flow to its wealth container. We will now look at the most common of these obstacles to moneymaking, which are **belief systems, relationships, unfinished business, attitude and unsuccessful actions.**

2

Belief Systems

How does your thinking contain your wealth? Where does your thinking leak?

Leaks and blocks

Leaks and blocks, as I mentioned before, relate to my second law of wealth creation – *Clean Flows*. The first law is *Clear Intent*, which was covered in the section on container. Clean Flows relates to many areas of life, as we saw in the section on flow. Here we will look at the main causes of leaks or blocks in our life and wealth flow, and in our wealth container.

We are still working with the image of an underground pipe along which money and energy flow towards your destination. If your pipe leaks, your container will never be full. If your container leaks it will also never be full. Apart from leaks, there may also be blocks and they, too, will cramp the piping and restrict flow, if not stop it altogether.

There are many things that stop or slow down money flow. Let's look at the first of these: belief systems.

Belief systems

Your belief system about money and its attainment (as well as your belief (or not) in miracles and wonders – or 'the impossible') will determine not only how big your container is, it will also determine if you have a container at all. In order to contain more money in your life, you need to believe different things from what you believe right now. Firstly, you need to examine and reconfigure your belief system around money. As long as you believe that money is bad, or that it is hard to come by, or that you only want 'enough' of it, you will be unable to get the money flowing. To contain more money, you need a bigger container. To create a bigger container, you need to be able to believe in a bigger container – that it can exist, that you can create it, and that you can contain it. (Yes, you contain the container.)

Here is a pretty simple, unrelated, but very apt example. Our kitchen fridge was rather small as it went back to the days before we had children. However, it seemed to fit in everything we needed quite well, if sometimes it was a bit of a squeeze. Some time later we bought a fridge which was twice as big, with a freezer at least four times bigger. And guess what? After a very short time, this fridge was chock-a-block too, so that we now wonder if we need a two-door one. To contain more, you need a bigger container. Let's get back to belief systems.

A belief system around money that is not in resonance with creating more wealth will shrink your container and diminish your money flow. A belief system is a complex arrangement of interlinked views, data, hearsay, opinions, and emotions around a certain subject which have been linked together in the mind under a certain section – in this case, money. And this linking began many, many years ago with your first conscious memory of money. To that were added things people said that you took on, your own experiences and conclusions drawn, as well as lessons you have learnt or think

157

you've learnt along the way.

To change your beliefs around money, you need to change your mind. This is a lot easier than we think, if we approach it with the right attitude. First you need to confront, or see what is there, then you simply have to say something like, 'No, I don't really believe that any more – this is what I believe.' You may need to do it more than once, but the mind is fickle and, with the right incentive, it loves to flit about all over the place. This is a benefit in this case. It is good to cultivate the ability to change your mind. Because, let's face it, what is a thought anyway, that we should place so much value on it? Let it go if it does not suit you. Just let it go. It's as easy as that.

Letting go of thoughts and beliefs only becomes difficult when we solidify them by making them Important. We make our thoughts Important when we isolate one and give it special treatment, like an honoured guest. We select it, invite it for tea, and ask its history – where it came from, what makes it tick, why it is there and what else it's attached to. Then, we find we may need to undergo therapy for a year to be able to reach the point where we can show this guest the front door. We can also simply let it go. It's easier and much more effective. Rather spend that year creating or filling up your wealth container.

Once you have looked at and let go of beliefs that do not support your new wealth vision, you need to create some new ones that do.

But let's start with where you are. My book *Money Alchemy* contains extensive processing to help you uncover what you think of money, the wealthy, and being wealthy. It is very worthwhile to do those exercises again here, in relation to this section on belief systems, as a prelude to the transformational work that follows, even if you have done them before.

Money Mind Map
Wealth Training Process

A mind map is a very useful tool for getting down thoughts around a subject freely, as they arise. It is also used as an aid to remembering. Here we will see what is there, and then transform it into something new. You will need: two pieces of large, blank, paper (A3 poster size), a box of coloured pens or crayons, and pen or pencil.

Give yourself a full hour for this work. This is work which will shift and change you on a very deep level. Allow the space and time for this. Take the phone off the hook, and be in a quiet space where you will not be interrupted. This is imperative for Part Three of the exercise in particular.

But first, *Set your Intent*!

In a clear, simple sentence, state your intent for this exercise. Why are you doing this? What are you hoping to achieve? It could be something like *'It is my intent to uncover and release any beliefs that do not resonate with wealth'*. You can rephrase into language that you are comfortable with.

Do not phrase your intent in the negative, as, for example, 'I don't want to think negative things about money any more'. This will only focus your mind on the beliefs you are trying to release. It would be better to state it like this: *'I intend to create beliefs that resonate with money.'*

Let's begin.

Part One – Seeing what Money Pattern is there
Wealth Training Process

1. Take one of the large pieces of blank paper (A3 – poster size) and write 'Old Money Thinking' on it.
2. Write down everything you can think of around the subject of money – what you think about it, how it makes you feel, old quotes and phrases, what you believe about money.
3. You can write in sections or you can write each item separately.
4. Allow any associations of image, texture, colour, smell, taste that arise to emerge, and jot them down, no matter how strange they may seem.
5. When you are finished, underline or circle items with a similar theme and join them together, using different coloured pens or crayons.
6. Try to see any patterns that may be there.
7. Isolate the three most important patterns or themes that have significance for you at this time.
8. Summarise these three themes into a sentence each.

9. Decide whether you want to keep or change these themes, beliefs or ideas.
10. Make the changes.
11. Write out the three new themes, patterns or beliefs you are embracing on your money journey.

Part Two – Creating a New Money Pattern
Wealth Training Process

1. Take the second piece of paper, and label it 'New Money Thinking'.
2. Write down on it the three new wealth supporting beliefs you created above. Circle each one, and keep lots of space around it.
3. Write down all the new, wealth empowering beliefs, attitudes, phrases, emotions you want to embrace associated with each one of the above themes, around each theme. It does not matter if they do not seem real or possible to you right now. You are looking at creating a reality in which these beliefs will come into being.
4. You can attach the words associated with each theme to that theme with different coloured lines.
5. Feel free to explore new themes, beliefs and patterns that may arise from any place on this New Money Thinking Map.
6. Continue to make new connections using coloured lines to join up related themes and ideas.

Part Three – Transforming the Energy
Advanced Wealth Transformation Process

You will need at least half an hour of uninterrupted quiet time for this part of the exercise. You cannot rush this exercise, so having extra time would be useful.

1. Sit on a comfortable chair at a table that can accommodate both of the above Money Maps.
2. Place the Old Money Thinking Map on the table on the left, and the New Money Thinking Map next to it on the right, with a gap between the two maps.
3. Enter a quiet and still place, using deep rhythmic breathing to still

your body and mind.

4. Focus your intent on transforming the thought energy associated with your old beliefs into thought energy that will feed your new belief structure about money.

5. Shut your eyes and be still.

6. State your intent that this work is done under the protection of the Divine and invite your image of the Divine to protect you while you do this work of energy transformation. Invite your image of the Divine to take a seat within your heart.

7. Imagine a warm fire burning between the two maps. See it glowing in your mind's eye, and hear it crackle merrily.

8. Now imagine the thought energy from all the lines and patterns and ideas on the first, old map pouring into the fire as a column of dark grey smoke. Use your breathing as you do this to breathe in the beliefs and breathe them out deeply into the fire. Breathe in and out through the heart.

9. Should you experience any physical or emotional discomfort, continue breathing out until the feeling is gone. This is important. Do not stop in the middle of such a process.

10. As the grey smoke pours into the fire it becomes clarified in a violet flame and emerges clear and golden, pouring into the New Money Thinking Map.

11. Consciously, using your breathing and intent, direct the clear golden light into your New Money Thinking Map.

12. Now breathe in this golden energy, through your heart, into every part of your body, as well as your mind and fill yourself with the thought energy of positive wealth flow.

13. Finally, allow the golden thought energy of being wealthy to flow out of you from your heart into the world, attracting more of the same to you, bringing back all good things to you.

15. When all the grey smoke has been transformed, take up the first map in your mind's eye and throw it into the fire.

16. Thank the fire and watch as it goes out and is gone.

17. Thank the Divine for the protection.

18. End the transformation by physically burning the Old Mind Map in a safe way.

This is an extremely powerful energetic transformation. It is perfectly safe to do, if you follow the instructions closely and exactly.

The most important thing to remember is to continue transforming the grey smoke, continue breathing out into the fire whatever emotion or physical discomfort arises, until all the grey smoke, emotion, and discomfort is gone. No matter how long this takes.

After this exercise, expect to feel tired. Have a rest and take it easy. Do not continue with any other energetic transformational processes for at least a week. Two weeks is better, or even longer, depending on how you feel. Some of you may feel energised and elated – even so, you should still take a break. Do not do any of the other transformational exercises (writing, drawing, reflecting) either until at least a week has gone by. But do, do the grounding below.

Putting your Money where your Process is

It is always a good idea to ground any energetic transformation in the physical world. This can be seen as the planting of a seed, or utilising the good energy you have created in a tangible way. You do this by directing your intent through inspired action.

A great deal of energy was generated and redirected in your energetic templates in the previous exercises. By properly grounding this energy in the physical world, you help fulfil and develop the new beliefs and attitudes you intend to cultivate. Through taking physical action in the world you impress your intent upon the universe, and you imprint upon yourself the fact that what you are doing is a process of real, tangible wealth transformation. In effect, action is what sets the wheels of all intent and transformation rolling.

So, let us begin.

Part Four – Grounding the New Energy
Wealth Training Process

As soon as possible after doing the energetic transformation above, do the following:

1. Think of something in your life that is important to do, resolve or act upon right now. This can be anything from the sale of an asset you may have been putting off, to applying for a job, starting a new business, or to asking for forgiveness. It is something that has been

162

occupying your attention for some time but that you have not had the time, energy, or resources to complete.

2. Put your intent on using the energy generated above for the successful completion of this task.
3. Perform the action with the full force of the energy now at your disposal.
4. Complete the task.
5. See this action as a symbolic act of grounding the energetic transformation and acting as new seeds that will sprout all the new attitude and feelings you have created.

Creating new beliefs

Once you have integrated this experience, after a week or two, using the second New Money Thinking Mind Map, write a list of new beliefs and phrases around money that you want to integrate into your life. Start using them daily when you speak and, more importantly, when you think. If an old belief pops up, say 'no, *this* is what I now believe', and state the new belief. Don't fight the old, just allow it to pass, while focusing on the new.

It is from our beliefs that our attitudes and emotions arise. This is an important thing to remind ourselves of from time to time. That one tiny little misplaced thought can create an entire chain of associated beliefs, with accompanying emotions, which then act as beacons of energy, attracting to us something completely different from what we want.

Take care of what beliefs you unwittingly cultivate. Be aware of which opinions, phrases and humorous messages you allow to inhabit your mind. Take note, and exercise choice. Above all, do not identify with your thoughts.

Entertaining beliefs about wealth and your creation of it that are not wholesome will weaken the fabric of your container or put holes in it, or will puncture the piping that carries your wealth flow to you. On the other hand, not believing in the impossible will make your container vanish altogether. Because, after all, what is this container but an ephemeral dream that you are coaxing into reality?

Believing the impossible

To create a life with lots of money, no debt, a beautiful home, or a successful business, to bring into being a cherished dream and make it real, to contain wealth, you need first the ability to imagine.

Imagination is more important than knowledge, said Einstein. And indeed, without the ability to imagine, nothing can be achieved. Budgets and financial planning, goal setting and positive affirmations will really not help you.

Imagining is more than merely thought, and it is even more than creating a picture in your mind. Imagining involves the creation of a reality not yet born, and infusing it with such feeling, such colour, such passion, such vision and belief, that you cause it to come into being.

This is not positive thinking. This is connecting with a part of you that is bigger than you imagine. It is tuning in to a certain frequency that extends beyond the frequency of the 'real' and the 'possible'. And to do it you need to lighten up and play. You also need to embrace the mysteries of life. You need to make room in your life for miracles and wonders, because without them no wealth has ever been created. And therefore, logically speaking, those who cannot believe in the unknowable will never prosper. (Sounds like a Bible verse, doesn't it?)

> *The grown-ups to be sure will not believe you when you tell*
> *them that*
> Antoine De Saint-Exupéry from *The Little Prince*

Tales of mystery and imagination

When I was young, my father told me amazing tales of the unexplained – of Houdini, Yuri Geller, spoon bending, mind reading, hypnotism, even the possibility of going to other planets!

And at the end of every story my father would spread out his hands and shrug his shoulders in that characteristically continental way. 'What do we know, my child, what do we know?' he would say. He never tried to explain or rationalise. He never went into whether any of the stories was possible or real. He merely left the doors of possibility open for me.

So it is that I grew up believing that anything is possible. And this is, without a doubt, the single most important secret of my success in business and moneymaking. I believe. I believe that I can do anything! I believe anything is possible. And this belief is what has led me through all the dire straits that I have faced along my wealth journey.

Let me put it another way. When it's a few days before month end, in the third month of your new business, and you have rent and staff to pay and no money in the bank, what will help you?

Logic will tell you it's over, you'd best call the bank for an overdraft. Logic will tell you it is not possible to get in the funds in such a short space of time.

Believing that anything is possible, however, will tell you it can be done, that it will be done. Miracles and wonders will tell you it's not a problem. The impossible will make it happen, if you only believe in it. And I can assure you that belief in the impossible is the most dependable source of creation that you can find in times of trouble. It has always worked for me.

Indeed, when we were in the third month of our new business in portfolio management, having spent our meagre start-up capital on start-up and paying staff and rent up to this point, we lurched towards month end with no idea how we would meet our overheads. But we believed, and we held on to hope with both hands, and we laughed (probably a little too loudly), and we held the doors of possibility open, and we *knew* we would make it.

And, lo and behold, literally a few days before the weekend and month end – it was in fact a Tuesday – in walked a client. He literally walked into the office. Now this was in itself most unusual. Prospective clients do not usually just walk in to hand over their portfolios for management. And this was not just any client. This was the first client I had ever signed up on the first day I had ever gone out as an investment consultant while working for a boss several years before. He had traced me, and he appeared, saying he wanted me to manage his funds!

To say this was a miracle would be a real understatement! There was no logical way we could have thought up or planned this amazing solution. To allow for such a bizarre and wondrous thing to take place would necessitate going into the realms of the impossible. There is simply no other way it could have been done. And here is the most important bit – if we had not believed in the impossible, it would never have happened. This, I know for sure.

Cultivating a new belief

Cultivating a new belief system, in this case about money, is the same as cultivating anything else – a garden, a new relationship, a new skill. It requires attention, practice, and patience. We recognise this fact when it comes to things more tangible than thought. We say, yes, of course I will need to practise for at least an hour every day to learn this new skill of piano playing or tennis or to get fit. Naturally I do not expect my relationship to flourish if I only see my partner once a month. And I know I must dig and compost and water and tend my garden before I can expect to see the results of all this hard work I am putting into it. And, yes, I expect all of this to take time.

We know and acknowledge the time, effort and practice associated with cultivating anything, except thought. When it comes to changing the mind, and cultivating a new belief system, we somehow expect that it should be different, instantaneous, something you get or you don't. Much like wealth creation itself, we think it's something you are born inherently able to do or not. This is not true. To create a new belief system about money, one that will result in the creation of a new energetic pattern in your life, one that will result in a new way of being and a new resonance, one that will in turn result in the seemingly effortless attraction of more wealth in your life, takes much practice.

What makes things a little more challenging is that the practice of changing a belief is not the sort of practice that we usually relate to as practice. It is not something we 'do' as much as it is a quality of attention and of being present in our thinking. It is a quality of being.

Changing your mind

Apart from practice, cultivating a new belief requires the ability to

166

change your mind, and the humility and good nature to admit to being wrong. This, too, is something you become better at with practice. It is good to be able to change your mind about something or someone – I try to do it as a part of my daily practice. Rather than seeing a change of mind as some sort of failing, I look upon it as a change of heart, particularly when it come to judgements (usually prematurely made about others). I always 'change my mind' out loud, in the presence of a witness (usually Shaun, my husband). I sometimes will do it in the course of giving an unconsidered opinion which, while I think about it in the course of talking, I realise is incorrect.

How often we feel compulsively compelled to defend a word spoken in haste, or an opinion based on too little thought or proof. And what a burden this is, because deep inside we know we should just drop it and say, 'You know what, I think I've changed my mind about Jim. I thought he was unfriendly, but I realise he's actually shy.' Okay, let me do a juicier one. How about: 'I was wrong to dislike Mary because I thought she was making eyes at my boyfriend, she's just a naturally flirty girl, and I think I now like her.'

It's fantastic practice to cultivate the ability to change your mind through allowing the possibility of being wrong, or even just because you can.

'You know I've changed my mind about Sam. He used to get on my nerves, but now I like him.'

'Why?'

'I don't know, must be the moon.'

Allow yourself that. Give yourself permission to change your mind.

We are taught that changing our mind is a bad thing. Well, it is not. Learn to say 'I think I'm going to change my mind about that' as if doing so is the greatest virtue – because it is. What are thoughts really, anyway, that we should think them so very important?

In conclusion

Your belief system around money, the wealthy, and being wealthy together with the accompanying emotions that these belief systems arouse, can warp or destroy your wealth container. In fact, your beliefs around money can prevent you from creating a container in the first place, and without a container, you cannot contain money.

To be able to create a wealth container you must be open to dreaming and to believing in the improbable. To cultivate this ability, allow yourself to dream in spectacular detail, consort with little children, expand your thinking, and lighten up!

Belief systems create patterns. These patterns resonate at a certain frequency. To change frequency you must change the pattern. Creating new beliefs about money, changing your mind, re-patterning for wealth, and using your new beliefs and mottos on a regular basis will significantly alter your wealth frequency.

> *On average, an infant laughs nearly 200 times a*
> *day, an adult only 12.*
> *Maybe they are laughing so much because they are*
> *looking at us*
> Laurence G Boldt from *Zen and the Art of Making a Living*

There is a world out there that is mysterious and magical and beyond comprehension. We do not need to know or explain its mysteries, because the minute we do, we limit them. And when we try to limit the mysterious and the magical we are no longer working in the realm of miracles, where anything can happen.

3

Attitude

Do you have a healthy attitude towards wealth? How wholesome is your attitude to life?

Attitude

Although attitude can be seen as the sum total effect of all the other elements under leaks and blocks, which together create the overall resonance of a person, we will cover attitude here, instead of at the end, as it has things in common with belief systems. Whereas the other elements – unfinished business, relationships, and unsuccessful actions – can create leaks and blocks in your container or wealth flow, attitude, like belief systems, can warp your container, or even destroy it altogether.

In simple terms, your attitude is the emotional essence arising from your belief systems which colours everything you see, experience, and do. It has long been my belief that with the right attitude, you can do anything. And on that basis, I have often employed people with little or no experience or qualification over others more highly qualified and experienced, on the simple basis of attitude. I believe that all other things can be taught, but I cannot teach someone how to have the right attitude. Which I am about to try to do here . . . I can only hope you have the right attitude to changing your attitude. If you're this far into the book I imagine you must have! So, for me, the right attitude always takes precedence.

What is the right attitude? Well it's one of those indefinable things. Nonetheless, everyone understands instantly what is meant by right or good attitude versus wrong or bad attitude (except, usually, the person whose attitude is lacking . . .).

There are two aspects of right attitude, the general and the specific. It is not an exaggeration to say that broadly speaking someone with an overall good attitude will have a good attitude towards his or her relationship, job, work, money, and children; whereas a generally bad attitude will cloud all areas of life in a similar way.

In specific terms, particularly where it is job related, the right attitude for a funeral attendant will not be the same as that of the head of a corporation, though either may have an overall good or bad attitude towards life as a whole.

Getting specific about money, it may seem obvious to say that you will never attract it if you have the wrong attitude about it, or towards it. Because attitude not only colours everything you see; it is also the magnet that you carry around with you throughout life. It is a large magnet, very powerful, like an enormous shield (actually it's a field . . .) around your body attracting everything in tune with your attitude and resonance towards you.

We will not go into how attitude comes to be here – that is another subject. For the purposes of what we are doing, which is looking at blocks and leaks relevant to containing money, all we need to do is coolly examine our attitude to moneymaking and change it where necessary. We need to look at our attitude as it is, right now, lightly, with compassion, and without judgement or blame.

It does not matter how it came to be so. When you discover your ship is leaking in the middle of a storm, you do not sit down and go into therapy or debate or argument over what caused the leak and how it could have been prevented (not unless you're in government, that is). What you do is assess the leak, fix it, and make sure there are no other leaks. That is the first order of business in a leaking ship, and that is the first order of business here.

In the following wealth training exercises, we will shine the light of our consciousness on attitude. First we will examine attitude towards wealth using various tools. Attitude is a collective nuance, an emotion, the paint which colours our looking glass. It is a predisposition towards something – an essence of many factors – ephemeral, hard to pinpoint or define. However, in order to change it, we need to find the underlying components, the parts that make up the whole. So, after reflecting on our attitude, we will deconstruct it into underlying assumptions and emotions, with a view to changing some of those components and creating a new whole – one which resonates with the creation of wealth.

If you cannot do this now, do, do, come back soon! Meanwhile, keep reading.

Part One: Illuminating my Attitude to Wealth
Wealth Training Process

A. Write for two minutes on each prompt. Write clearly, honestly and as it appears on paper. No one will read this but you. Allow yourself the freedom of truth. If you run out of words, repeat the prompt. Remember, we are looking at attitude, not thinking or beliefs. Focus your attention on feelings, rather than mental replay. Attitude is how you feel and how that feeling translates itself into, well, an attitude . . .

1. Life is ....
2. Beggars on the street highlight ....
3. Those more fortunate than me make me feel ....
4. When I am given an unexpected favour I imagine ....
5. When I do a favour for someone I expect ....
6. When I have a problem, my first impulse is to ....
7. I feel world catastrophes are ....
8. Money should ....

9. My attitude towards being wealthy is ....

- Once you are finished, read through and underline key words and phrases with a different coloured pen.
- Capture the overall mood and emotion of your response to each prompt and write it next to each prompt in a circle, for example, judgemental, positive, blaming, optimistic. Be real. Be honest. No one will see this but you.
- Capture the underlying assumption underpinning each attitude. List these assumptions. For example:
    1. I assume that people who are richer than me are not as spiritual as I am.
    2. I assume that people who help have ulterior motives.
- Extract the key element underpinning each assumption. What is at its core? For example (for the examples above):
    1. Possibly Arrogance/Ego
    2. Possibly Fear or Lack of Trust
    There is no right or wrong answer here; it all depends on where the spotlight shines for you.

B. For the next week, observe yourself compassionately in your everyday life, as if you are watching a divine comedy. That means you are aware of your divinity and perfection, yet you indulgently witness the folly and foibles of being human. In other words, observe lightly without judgement. Observe your attitude, especially around little things. Take notes if you need to. Capture the essence of your attitude. Allow yourself to be surprised.
    (a) List attitude that you wish to retain and cultivate – that which expands you, life and wealth. Keep this as a separate list for the exercise on 'Transforming Attitude to Wealth'.
    (b) List attitude that you wish to transform – that which contracts you, life, and wealth.
    (c) Capture the underlying assumption underpinning each attitude. List these assumptions.
    (d) Capture the underlying emotion underpinning each attitude. List these emotions.
    (e) Extract the key element underpinning each assumption. What is at its core?

C. Do this one only if you have some truly trusted friends, mentors or teachers. It is a good idea to avoid asking your partner for input. Ask two people you truly trust to each give you three words which they feel best describe your attitude to wealth and money (*in their opinion*). If you know this will cause you angst, do not do it. Do not ask them for further input. Coolly assess the words and extract the emotions and assumptions that underlie them.

D. Draw a border around the edge of a new, blank piece of A3 paper, and label it 'Old Attitudes about Money'. Write all the emotions, assumptions, aspects and key elements underpinning your attitude to wealth, as revealed by the exercises above inside the border. You can arrange them in any way you like. Make any connections you need to make, using different coloured pens.

E. Draw any conclusions you need to draw, and list any changes you wish to undertake, and any action you want to perform.

Cultivating right attitude requires practice. In Buddhism we speak of right speech, right action, right livelihood, and so on. Just contemplating the idea of that is most useful. It will mean different things to different people. Cultivating right attitude requires practice, patience, and a willingness to change.

Part Two: Transforming my Attitude to Wealth
Wealth Training Process

A. Spend two minutes on each prompt. Allow yourself to write freely, from the heart.

1. When I feel totally healthy, wealthy, and wise I can ....
2. When I feel powerful and safe in the world I can ....
3. In my ideal world I am ....
4. When I feel free to do whatever I want to, I will ....
5. When I am living my ideal life, I would like to do .... for others.
6. When I am extremely wealthy I will have ....
7. When I feel extremely wealthy, I feel ....about money. I feel money is ....

8. I celebrate the joy of wealth through ....
9. I realign my attitude to wealth to include .... (List nine wealth enhancing attitudes, including feelings, you would like to adopt.)
10. I embrace the following wealth enhancing beliefs .... (List three wealth enhancing beliefs you would like to embrace.)
11. I commit to the following successful actions of abundance .... (List three actions you will commit to performing regularly, as part of your celebration of wealth.)
12. I am grateful for the following in my life today .... (List eleven joyful, life enhancing things that you are grateful for.)

- When you are finished, read through and underline key words and phrases with a different coloured pen or crayon.
- Capture the overall mood and emotion from each response and list this in a circle next to each prompt.
- Capture the underlying assumption underpinning each response. List these assumptions.
- Extract the key element underpinning each assumption. What is at its core?

B.1 Draw a border around the edge of a new, blank piece of A3 paper, and label it 'NEW Attitudes about Money'. Write all the emotions, assumptions, aspects and key elements underpinning the new attitude you want to cultivate towards wealth, as revealed by the exercise above, inside the border. You can arrange them in any way you like. Make any connections you need to using different coloured pens.

B.2 Add the list of 'attitudes you wish to retain and cultivate' from the previous section (Part One: 'Illuminating My Attitude to Wealth' B (a)).

B.3 Draw any conclusions you need to draw, and list any changes you wish to undertake, and execute any actions you want to perform as a result of this knowledge.

You now have all the elements of your OLD attitude as well as all the elements of the NEW wealth enhancing attitude you wish to cultivate. The following energetic transformation will transform the energy locked in the old attitude into energy that can be used for your new attitude. This is a powerful process. Treat it with respect.

Part Three: Transforming the Energy
Advanced Wealth Transformation Process

You will need at least half an hour of uninterrupted quiet time for this part of the exercise. You cannot rush this exercise, so having extra time would be useful.

1. Sit on a comfortable chair at a table that can accommodate both the OLD Attitude Map and the NEW Attitude Map from the wealth training processes above.
2. Place the old attitude map on the table on the left, and the new one next to it on the right, with a gap between the two maps.
3. Enter a quiet and still place, using deep rhythmic breathing to still your body and mind.
4. Focus your intent on transforming the thought energy associated with your Old Attitude into thought energy that will feed your New Attitude about money.
5. Shut your eyes and be still.
6. State your intent that this work is done under the protection of the Divine and invite your image of the Divine to protect you while you do this work of energy transformation. Invite your image of the Divine to take a seat within your heart.
7. Imagine a warm fire burning between the two maps. See it glowing in your mind's eye, and hear it crackle merrily.
8. Now imagine the thought energy from all the lines and patterns and ideas on the first, old map pouring into the fire as a column of dark grey smoke. Use your breathing as you do this to breathe in the attitudes and breathe them out deeply into the fire. Breathe in and out through the heart.
9. Should you experience any physical or emotional discomfort, continue breathing out until the feeling is gone. This is important. Do not stop in the middle of such a process.
10. As the grey smoke pours into the fire it becomes clarified in a violet flame and emerges clear and golden, and pours into the New Attitude Map.
11. You breathe in this golden energy, through your heart, into every part of your body, as well as your mind, and fill yourself with the attitude and feeling of positive wealth flow.

12. Finally you allow the golden energy of the attitude and feeling of being wealthy to flow out of you from your heart into the world, bringing back all good things to you.
13. When all the grey smoke has been transformed, take up the first map in your mind's eye and throw it into the fire.
14. Thank the fire and watch as it goes out and is gone.
15. Thank the Divine for the protection.
16. End the transformation by physically burning the Old Attitude Map in a safe way.

This is an extremely powerful energetic transformation. It is perfectly safe to do, if you follow the instructions closely and exactly. The most important thing to remember is to continue transforming the grey smoke, continue breathing out whatever emotion or physical discomfort arises into the fire, until all the grey smoke, emotion, and discomfort is gone. No matter how long this takes.

After this exercise, expect to feel tired. Have a rest and take it easy. Apart from Grounding the New Energy (see below), do not continue with any other energetic transformational processes for at least a week. Two weeks is better, or even longer, depending on how you feel. Some of you may feel energised and elated – even so, you should still take a break. Do not do any of the other transformational exercises (writing, drawing, reflecting) either until at least a week has gone by. But do, do the grounding below.

Putting your money where your process is

It is always a good idea to ground any energetic transformation in the physical world. This can be seen as the planting of a seed, or utilising the good energy you have created in a tangible way. You do this by directing your intent through inspired action.

A great deal of energy was generated and redirected in your energetic templates in the previous exercises. By properly grounding this energy in the physical world, you help fulfil and develop the new beliefs and attitudes you intend to cultivate. Through taking physical action in the world you impress your intent upon the universe, and you imprint upon yourself the fact that what you are doing is a process of real, tangible wealth transformation. In effect, action is what sets the wheels of all intent and transformation rolling.

So, let us begin.

Part Four: Grounding the New Energy
Wealth Training Process

As soon as possible after doing the energetic transformation above, do the following:

1. Think of something in your life that is important to do, resolve or act upon right now. This can be anything from the sale of an asset you may have been putting off, to applying for a job, starting a new business, or to asking for forgiveness. It is something that has been occupying your attention for some time but that you have not had the time, energy, or resources to complete.
2. Put your intent on using the energy generated above for the successful completion of this task.
3. Perform the action with the full force of the energy now at your disposal.
4. Complete the task.
5. See this action as a symbolic act of grounding the energetic transformation and acting as new seeds that will sprout all the new attitude and feelings you have created.

When your attitude towards life and wealth radiates positive anticipation, joy, and optimism, your container is firm and solid. It can be relied upon to carry its contents. It can even help repair any little cracks and leaks as they occur. Polish your attitude. Practise radiating goodness from your heart and watch your container expand to embrace more.

A sound container is held together by the unity of forces that embody it. Your mind, heart, feelings and spirit must hold together one vision, one resonance, one field, in order for wealth to flow effortlessly towards you. More than any other element, the right attitude is the key to this success.

> *The greatest discovery of my generation is that a human being*
> *can alter his life by altering his attitude*
> William James

4

Incomplete Physical Cycles

What unfinished business drains your time, energy, and wealth?

Unfinished business

Unfinished business creates blocks which diminish your effectiveness and power which in turn significantly reduces your money flow. Unfinished business blocks the clear flow of energy and money along the unseen river of potential which is all around you. Unfinished business traps your attention, dispersing your power and will – you need all your attention fully in the present in order to create with skill and with ease. If your underground piping is blocked, no matter how much wealth there may be at source, it will never get to you.

Flow along a blocked pipe will eventually create tears and leaks in the piping. Leaking will further dissipate your energy and power. So it is best to remove blocks and repair leaks as soon as possible. Maintain your piping in good order. Ensure your plumbing works. If anything is leaking or blocked in other areas of your life, this will reflect on money also, because everything is connected.

There are three types of unfinished business: physical, mental and emotional. Of course the three are linked and overlap because everything is connected. We classify only for ease. Unfinished business relating to the **physical** encompasses **incomplete cycles, debt, and lack of attention.** On the **mental** front we are looking at patterns around **delivery, keeping your word, promises, hooked attention or mental congestion, and unexecuted intentions.** Unfinished business **emotionally** invariably has to do with self and others which we will deal with at length under the section on **Relationships** which follows.

At this stage you may feel quite overwhelmed and inclined to park this book and grab a chocolate bar or a drink. Go for it! Have a break, but do return. Dealing with unfinished business is such an enormous relief for your entire system, it is so fabulously energising and decongesting that I can absolutely promise you it will be the single most empowering thing you will do in a long time!

Let me tell you a story.

Once upon a time in the city, a suicidal patient phoned his therapist saying, 'I'm going to kill myself, I'm going to jump, right now!' The therapist was mid-session with another equally distraught patient and said, 'I can't deal with you right now, Johnny, but do me a favour. Please go and tidy out all your drawers, and then call me back. Can you do that, Johnny?' And Johnny said yes.

Well, apparently by the time all the drawers had been tidied, Johnny felt so much better, that he had no desire to jump at all. In fact, Johnny says that that little exercise may have well saved his life. I'm not sure if his name really was Johnny, it may have been Sue, but it's a true story.

It has been said that tidying out your work area can increase your production by as much as 25 per cent. I am not sure how this was worked out, but I do know for certain that creating order in your life will reap enormous rewards. A noticeable change will take place in your life when you tidy up your area or complete unfinished cycles. When you perform these acts with intent and attention, however, the results are significantly magnified!

There, I'm sure you are now ready to go, so let me issue a little warning. The following processes can create very powerful shifts, depending on your intent, where you are in your life, and what is happening for you at this time. Due to the 'clearing' nature of this subject, it is not uncommon to experience diarrhoea, flu-like symptoms, or other signs of physical clearing of your body after doing theses processes. For this reason, please do the following Wealth Training Exercises before a weekend. Of course not everyone is the same, and some people will experience a lightening of their system, like a burden lifted, and a great sense of well-being, with an increase in energy levels. Whatever your experience, these processes will clear the way for more wealth of every kind to flow into your container!

Clearing Unfinished Business
Unfinished Business on the Physical : *Incomplete Cycles, Debt, Lack of Attention*

Incomplete Physical Cycles

To properly understand what it means to have unfinished business, we need to re-look at cycles, a concept which was introduced in the section on flow.

A cycle is a series of actions which forms an activity or task. Cycles have a beginning, a doing part and an end. Until a cycle reaches and completes the end part, it is incomplete. It is good to reflect on which part of a cycle we get stuck on. Some people battle to start, others struggle to keep going, and some cannot finish. We need to do all three, in sequence, properly, to accomplish anything, and that includes moneymaking.

When we are looking at containing money, the start is the container. Without one we cannot start the cycle of containing money. There are many aspects to the 'doing' part, all to do with keeping the flows open and flowing towards your destination without diversion, blockages, or giving up. The 'end' part is arriving, receiving, actually holding that which has been created, embracing it without dropping it, or losing it, or letting go of it. The end is always the hardest part. But let's start at the beginning.

Let's look at the cycle of brushing teeth. The start involves taking a toothbrush and putting toothpaste on it. The middle is the act of brushing itself. The end is rinsing out and putting the toothbrush away.

If you are thinking of brushing your teeth but have not yet done it, this does not constitute an incomplete physical cycle. Your thinking may, if repeated often enough, create an unexecuted intention, but thought alone does not begin a physical cycle of action. When you pick up that toothbrush and add toothpaste, you are at the start of the cycle. If you now put the brush down and walk away, you have an incomplete cycle. If you brush only the bottom half of your mouth and get distracted, you have an incomplete cycle.

And, quite importantly for what we are doing, if you don't rinse out and put that brush away (no matter that your teeth are brushed), you have not completed the cycle. Of course, where the 'end' is, is a personal matter in the case of tooth brushing. Some people never put away their toothbrush. As long as you are quite clear that the end has been reached and the cycle is complete, that's fine. And only you can know this. How do you know? Well, when something is not finished it keeps tugging at your mind, you keep thinking about it, and this draws both attention and energy.

In the case of moneymaking, the end is when you have arrived, when you have attained your goal, when you have become that which you aspired to be, when your container is full. And yet, every end is a new beginning because moneymaking, like life, is a dynamic process, an ever constant turning, which cannot be stopped, for when it is death follows.

Let's get started then, with the clear intent of clearing away stuck energy, blocks and leaks, thereby making available increased flow of both energy and wealth!

Begin by stating this intent now.

Completing Physical Cycles
Wealth Training Process
Unblocking Wealth Flow

Each list has a limit on the number of items to be listed. You may be able to think of more. However, it is good to complete a shorter list of items and then do it again later if necessary, rather than to become overwhelmed by long 'to do' lists that may never get done. Some of the items on these lists may not be applicable to you – perhaps your drawers are already all neat and tidy, or you may not be in business.

Complete those items that are relevant to your life at this time.

1. List the top three priorities that come to mind when you think of unfinished business.
2. List up to seven incomplete physical cycles that need to be finished.
3. Record up to seven borrowed items you have not returned, or lent out that have not come back.
4. Think of three places in the home and three in your business that beg to be tidied or sorted out.

Inspired Action

1. Take inspired action!
2. Decide to end these cycles.
3. Set your intent on completing these cycles as a means of releasing blocks to wealth flow.
4. Take purposeful action.
5. Imagine your actions fixing leaks and unblocking the flow of wealth coming towards you.
6. Feel the increased energy and lightness that your action has created.
7. Expect wonderful things to happen!

We cannot do great things on this earth.
We can only do little things with great love
Mother Teresa

5

Clearing Debt

What debts need to be repaid? How does debt constrict your flow?

Living life in credit

This little word *debt* can create big problems. We live in a world that rewards and encourages debt. Debt reverses the natural order of the universe and contravenes the law of give to receive. If nature were to run according to modern day credit principles there would be chaos. Simply put, you absolutely have to sow before you can reap. You must plant seeds before you can harvest a crop. Debt reverses the abundant order of give and take, creating in its place a mentality of lack. Debt shrinks us, enslaves us, and takes away our power.

This is a very big subject that I will touch on only lightly here.

Mostly, I would like these words to raise your awareness and to plant the seeds for a life filled with assets. Debt has become a way of thinking that is rooted in the belief that 'you owe me'. It cultivates lack of charity and a closed heart. Debt promotes excessive and mindless consumerism. It encourages us to spend money before we've even earned it. Debt takes away our freedom and in so doing, it keeps us from pursuing our passion.

Set your intent to become free of debt. Better still, focus on living life in credit. It can be done. All you need to set the wheels in motion is a strong desire and a change in thinking and habit.

Once, many moons ago, I decided to end my debt. Obviously this decision was accompanied by an initial and necessary decrease in spending. I put all my credit and account cards away but one. Over time I paid each card off, cut it up, and returned it with a request to close the account. It was not easy. I could no longer just juggle things around or buy mindlessly at sales just because I could hand over an account card. One by one the cards were eliminated until I was left with only one, which is all I use, to this day, more than twenty years later. It is debited automatically each month against my bank account, and I really use it for convenience. Cutting up those credit cards was one of the greatest things I have ever done. Try it, and you'll see!

Apart from financial debt, there are many other, perhaps more insidious, forms of debt. We may become indebted to other people – owing them time, encouragement, gratitude, or attention. Or we may be putting others in our debt by doing too much for them, enslaving them, making them dependent and weak.

The cycle of give and receive is a two-way one. Both parts must function for the flow to continue. If we do not pick the fruits of our labour, the tree will become weak and eventually produce no fruit at all. We must receive as well as give, all in proper measure.

And then there is debt to self. What do we owe ourselves? Do we not owe it to our body to keep it healthy? Do we not owe it to ourselves to be happy, to be loved, to be fulfilling our potential, to be living our dreams? What do we owe ourselves?

Perhaps the most relevant aspect of any type of debt is that it creates weight. The weight is energetic, and though invisible, it can be quite clearly felt as weight on one's shoulders, a heaviness one carries in the head and a constriction around the heart. Others can see this invisible weight, and they can both see and feel when it is lifted. You look lighter, they say, and indeed you feel lighter too.

Let us now look at these other forms of debt and process around them remembering that when we clear something in one area of our lives, it will affect all others because everything is connected. And as we clear our debt, we will feel and appear lighter, our hearts will expand, and we will breathe easier too.

If you cannot do this exercise now, please come back to it later. It is a most important part of the wealth transformation process.

Clearing Debt – Releasing Life Force
Wealth Training Process

1. Sit in a comfortable chair and relax. Take some deep breaths and allow your thoughts to drift away.
2. When you feel relaxed and easy, think of Debt and write for two minutes on each prompt.
3. Allow your pen to write. Do not censor anything. You can burn the paper later if you wish.

A. Clearing Debt towards Others
(a) To whom am I indebted?
(b) What debts of gratitude do I have?
(c) What kindnesses do I need to acknowledge and repay?
(d) What unpaid debts of time and energy do I have towards others?
(e) What debts of encouragement, praise and attention do I owe?
(f) Whom do I refuse to acknowledge?
(g) To whom have I not said thank you?

When you are done, draw up a list of summarised items from your writing.

Inspired Action
1. Take inspired action!
2. Acknowledge, thank, repay, create, release, breathe, lighten up, open the flows of money.

3. Call, write a letter, change an attitude, simply acknowledge to yourself, undertake to give your time, energy, praise, attention.
4. Take action!
5. If anyone you wish to thank or acknowledge has passed on or you do not know where to reach them, you can still thank them. Either write them a letter, or imagine them sitting in a chair in front of you while you tell them what you feel.
6. Take action and clear the debt.
7. List any decisions you have taken and any new actions you wish to perform.
8. Acknowledge the increased energy and lightness this wealth training has produced.
9. Decide you are finished with these cycles and your debt to others is balanced.
10. Rejoice!

B. Clearing Indebtedness from Others

(a) Who is indebted to me? List up to seven items then answer the prompts (b) to (d) for each item.
(b) What do they owe me and why?
(c) How can they repay their debt to me?
(d) What needs to happen for me to consider this debt cycle complete?
(e) How do I put others in my debt?
(f) What is at the core of this pattern?
(g) How is this pattern reflected in other areas of my life?
(h) What do I need to do to change this pattern?
(i) What does the world owe me?
(j) What do my parents owe me?
(k) What do my children owe me?
(l) What does my partner owe me?
(m) What does my company owe me?

For each of (i) to (m) reflect on the following:
(1) Why?
(2) What assumption underlies this belief?
(3) What would need to happen for me to think differently?

Inspired Action

1. Take inspired action!
2. List any decisions you have taken and any actions you wish to perform.
3. Release, clear, create the conditions for repayment, end cycle.
4. Change your mind, change your attitude, change your assumptions.
5. Release, let go, forgive, release. Yes, you can!
6. Set your intent on the creation of new patterns. Create some new patterns of thought and action. Practise these new life affirming patterns.
7. Acknowledge the increased energy and lightness this wealth training has produced.
8. Decide you are finished with this cycle and the debt of others towards you is now balanced.
9. Rejoice!

C. Clearing Debt towards Self

1. What do I owe myself?
2. What else do I owe myself?
3. What else do I owe myself? Repeat the question seven times.

Underline important words and phrases with a different coloured pen. Summarise into one sentence.

Inspired Action

1. Take inspired action!
2. List any decisions you have taken and any actions you wish to perform.
3. Change your mind, change your attitude, change your assumptions.
4. Repay the debt to yourself – make things right.
5. Set your intent on the creation of new patterns. Create some new patterns of thought and action. Practise these new life affirming patterns.
6. Acknowledge the increased energy and lightness this wealth training has produced.

7. Decide you are finished with this cycle and your debt towards self is balanced.
8. Rejoice!

Once you have completed this section, you need to acknowledge what an amazing job you have just done! People go through an entire lifetime without even touching on what you have just cleared!

You have cleared debt towards self and others, and released indebtedness towards you. You have balanced out the energetic debt in your life! Well done!

You will soon find a strange and curious thing happening in your life. Soon, very soon, you will notice, somehow, in some strange way, that the financial debt in your life may start to reverse itself. You may discover a new willingness and ability to reduce your spending, a windfall of some kind may appear. One way or another, the balancing of energetic debt in your life will reflect on the physical too – just wait and see!

Meanwhile, celebrate your achievement by grounding it in action!

- Take time out and have a long bath by candlelight
- Watch the sunset with the one you love (and that could be you!)
- Have a fabulous dinner with lover or friends
- Have an early night with a good book and a box of chocolates
- Dance the night away
- Celebrate!

For all time is here, now, In our awakening
Ben Okri from *Mental Fight*

6

Paying Attention – Getting Focus

Is your attention on things that matter? Are you focused on wealth?

Unfinished business – paying attention – getting focus

Lack of attention is the result of not being in the present and of having too much of a cluttered mind (and may the one without blame here cast the first stone . . .). Learning to be in the present is of course what much of our life journey is all about. It is the focus of many religions, most meditation practices, and many transformational processes. So it may sound like a bit of a tall order to say let's come into the present, let's pay attention, let's practise mindfulness. Let us rather say that we will try. Let us say we will put our attention on it, if you'll forgive the pun.

Paying attention, practising mindfulness, is a matter of practice.

The more you practise, the better you get. At the root of mindfulness are intent and the willingness to do it. Without this you will not practise at all. Willingness contains the word *will* because without the will, well, you know what they say, there will be no way. Set your intent, exercise your will and practise.

The more attention you pay to everything, the more present and aware you are, the more conscious you will become. Why do you think that God is both omnipotent and omniscient? To be omniscient you need to able to have your attention on every single grain of sand, every single atom, every single quark across time and space, all at once. Quite a tall order. Makes what we want to do not such a tall order after all.

To know something you must pay attention. To see something you must pay attention. To change something you must pay attention. To make money you must pay attention. Has that got your attention?

Good.

Lack of attention can result in many incomplete cycles accumulating all around you. Though you may turn a blind eye towards things that need your attention, your mind records everything, and a part of you knows. The incomplete cycles create clutter and take up energy. Your mind is distracted and unable to focus properly. Without proper focus, you cannot create. Incomplete cycles caused by lack of attention cause blocks in the flow of your wealth energy. They also disperse your wealth focus away from your container, dissipating wealth through the various leaks along the way.

Let us look now at fixing some of these leaks and blocks in the following wealth training. *You know by now that you can come back later but, just for once, can you not stay and do the exercise?*

Paying Attention – Cultivating Mindfulness I
Wealth Training Process

Set your intent on the desire to cultivate and develop your attention. Set your intent on completing any cycles caused by lack of attention, for the purpose of strengthening your wealth container. Using the following prompts, write for two minutes on each.

1. What am I not paying attention to? List seven things.
2. Which/who of the following needs my attention?
   (a) My car/house/appliances/garden?
   (b) My health/diet/emotions/gifts/talent?
   (c) My plans/future/dreams?
   (d) My partner/children/parents/relatives/friends?
   (e) A stranger/charity/worthwhile cause?
3. What nagging thoughts do I have? List seven things that recur regularly.
4. What do I keep putting off doing?
   (a) Seeing a professional?
   (b) Setting up an appointment?
   (c) Talking to someone?
   (d) Fixing up my house/clothes/garage?
5. What takes up most of my thinking?

Underline important words and phrases with a different coloured pen. Summarise into one sentence.

Inspired Action
1. Take inspired action!
2. List any decisions you have taken and any actions you wish to perform.
3. Set your intent on living mindfully in the present. Pay attention.
4. Acknowledge the increased energy and lightness this wealth training has produced.
5. Decide you are finished with this cycle and your attention is here, now.
6. Rejoice!

Paying Attention – Cultivating Mindfulness II
Wealth Training Process

Whole books are written on the subject of mindfulness – some of these are noted at the end of this one.

What follows are a few simple acts you can perform daily. These will greatly increase your ability to pay attention and to be in the present.

1. When you next get home, pause outside your front door and look closely around you. Notice things you do not normally notice. What do you see?
2. When you wake up in the morning, pay attention to your body. How does it feel?
3. When your partner or children next talk to you, stop everything and really listen. What are they saying?
4. Walk barefoot for three minutes inside or out. Walk slowly and feel each part of your foot touching the earth.
5. Eat a piece of fruit slowly, savouring every mouthful. Taste, smell, feel and hear what you are eating.

Practise these as often as you can. Create your own practices in mindfulness.

Putting it all together

In this section we have looked at unfinished business on the physical. We have examined the make-up of a cycle and processed unfinished business in the area of incomplete cycles, debt, and lack of attention.

We have completed cycles, balanced debt, and focused our attention. We have celebrated and rejoiced in these achievements. We have cleared energy flow, and strengthened our wealth container, repairing leaks and blocks.

Surely wealth is, even as we speak, flowing towards us!

Once inner silence is attained, everything is possible
Carlos Castaneda from *The Wheel of Time*

7

Putting the Power Back into Words

**Do you say what you mean, and mean what you say?
Does your word have power?**

Unfinished business on the mental
1. Delivery – keeping your word, promises
2. Hooked attention and mental congestion
3. Unexecuted intentions

Delivery – keeping your word, promises
Putting the power back into words

Do you deliver? Can you be relied upon to do as you say? What is your word worth? Do you do what you promise?

When I was in fund management, the saying 'my word is my

bond' was synonymous with trading on the stock exchange. When you phoned a stockbroker and placed an order, often for millions, it was totally understood by both parties that this was the case. Never mind that you confirmed in writing later. Once the order was taken, that broker was on the floor dealing. Never mind that by the time you sent confirmation the stock could have plummeted or reached new highs. In fact, before my time, before emails and faxes, the telephone call to the broker served as both order and confirmation. Your word was your bond. End of chat.

We live in a world where our word only applies in certain contexts or formats or under certain conditions. If someone says something but does not put it in writing, it has no validity. If a reference number was not assigned to someone's promise, then that promise is meaningless. Even if someone agrees that he said something (which was not written down or assigned a reference number), he can later argue as to what he really meant when he said that something. Legal experts intricately arrange words to ensure the exactness of meaning which is later debated in court.

In all of this confusion around words, our *word* has become lost. Can you say 'my word is my bond'? No matter what, anywhere, any time? That is the question. And I hope the answer is 'yes', because if you want the universe to deliver, then you'd better be able and willing to deliver too. If you want to believe that when you get to your wealth container it will be full, then you'd better also be someone who keeps their word. If you want to believe in the impossible, and in miracles, and in promises of a wealthier future, then you'd better be able to deliver on your own promises first. Because that's the way it works.

Now I know that in the movies the mega wealthy guys are sleazy, no-good, lying, dishonest, non-deliverers who cheat and connive at every turn. But, hey, it's only a movie. And if you want to believe that the good guys also get rich (which they do) then you'd best perfect your delivery.

Simply put: As you give, so you shall receive. If you deliver, the world will deliver. If you keep your word, others will do so also. If you keep your promises, so will the universe. Love is not so unconditional after all . . . (Of course, I'm joking, maybe . . .)

The fact is that the more you radiate integrity, the more power is contained in your word, the more you will attract to you those of like resonance. The others will be there also, but they have nothing to do with you. And, yes, every now and again stuff happens, and there are always exceptions. But, as a rule, if you maintain your integrity and your word is true, that is what you too will receive from the world (with an odd exception here and there).

Lack of delivery, not keeping your word, constricts both your piping and your container. It also constricts your heart. It makes you cold and destroys faith and the belief in magic. Because if you cannot believe yourself (which is the case if you do not keep your word), whom can you believe? If you cannot trust yourself to keep your promises, how can you trust anyone else to? That is the computation that your mind sets up, and over time you come to believe it. Then, not only do you lose your faith, which is the worst possible thing you can lose (except for your mind perhaps – though many would argue that's a mighty fine thing to lose too), but you lose the power of your word.

Sticks and stones

Let us look at the power of the word. The saying that 'sticks and stones can break your bones but words will never harm you' is in fact the wrong way round. We know that 'In the beginning was the Word' – *Logos* in Greek – and we know that God spoke and said 'Let there be Light, and there was Light'. As God spoke, so it was, so it came to pass. We also know that 'as above, so below; as below, so above'. That means as we speak, so it is. Whatever we keep saying does come to pass.

Words have power. That power is contained in the energy infused into those words over time, together with the energy and intent we pour into those words in the moment we speak them. The more clear, directed, and unobstructed the energy we can put into our words, the more power they contain, and the more potent they become.

When you speak on a subject you feel strongly about, your words sizzle, they attract and mesmerise the audience. This power is a combination of energy and truth. To keep your word true, keep your word true.

To maintain the power of your word speak only truth – no matter what – honour your promises, and deliver.

Unfinished business relating to your not keeping your word results in constriction of your piping and container. Everything shrinks, including your world view. To open up to trust and to receiving all good things, put the power back into your word.

We will do this now by completing incomplete cycles around promises, and opening up the space to the power of truth.

PS: There is no such thing as a white lie!

Unfinished Business – Putting the Truth back into Words
Wealth Training Process

First, set your intent on putting the power back into your word through these processes. Also affirm that this processing will release constriction in your wealth flow and your heart. Do this now, in your own words, with intent.

For each question list three items. Once you have completed the exercise, you can do it again, with another three items or, if you are feeling sparky, try seven items. The important thing is not to become overwhelmed. *'Bean by bean, you fill up a sack'* (old proverb). Remember to do this process with compassion and no judgement.

1. List three recent promises made to others which you have not honoured. List the emotion that arises in you as you record each item, and circle it.
2. List three recent promises made to yourself, which you have not honoured. List and circle the emotion.
3. Record three things you said you'd do recently and did not. List the emotion, and circle it.
4. Record three things you said you'd do when you knew you would not. List the emotion and circle it.
5. Recall three times you did not keep your word. List the emotion that arises, and circle it.
6. List three old promises made to yourself, which you have not honoured. List and circle the emotion.
7. List three old promises made to others, which you have not hon-

oured. List and circle the emotion.

8. Recall three instances when you did not deliver. List and circle the emotion.

• Underline important words and phrases with a different coloured pen. Summarise into one sentence.

• Notice the dominant emotion which arises with each.

Inspired Action

1. Take inspired action!
2. List any decisions you have taken and any actions you wish to perform. Do them.
3. Item by item and list by list, complete these cycles. Do what you said you would do. Honour your promises. Deliver. Bring each cycle to completion.
4. If any of the items are now obsolete or irrelevant – for example, you promised yourself you'd date that guy or girl but you no longer want to, then cross them out and consider the cycle ended.
5. As you complete each cycle, tick it off on your list, and imagine the emotion associated with it becoming transformed into golden light which is infused into your word giving it power.
6. Acknowledge the increased energy and lightness this wealth training has produced.
7. Decide you are finished with this cycle, and your word has become infused with truth.
8. Set your intent on honouring the power of your word from this day forth.
9. Rejoice!

Make it a part of your ongoing practice to speak only truth from this day on, no matter what it takes. So be it. It is done. It's as easy as that. Well done!

And remember, if you slip up it's so easy to remedy – all you need to do is go back to the person involved and speak the truth. Say, 'I'm sorry, I don't know why I said I was ill yesterday; I just needed a day off.' It's really as easy as that.

The wonderful thing with this practice is that over time you will find it becomes physically impossible for anything but truth to come out of your mouth.

Truth has no colour
Kiki Theo

Hooked attention and mental congestion – releasing the mind

As mentioned before, the distinction between unfinished business on the physical, mental and emotional is not completely black and white. We have already dealt with hooked attention as it relates to things left undone or unseen. Here we will look at another form of hooked attention, that of the loop of repetitive internal dialogue.

This is an extremely draining form of unfinished business. It takes up time, energy, and creates the pattern of a truly never-ending cycle. It feeds on itself, and the more you go through the loop, the more the loop never ends.

We all know the scenario. You walk into the office, and there he/she is, smug as always, making you flustered as always. He/she smiles calmly as you drop your briefcase, and delivers one of his or her famous one-liners. To which you mumble something totally inane as you rush into your office trying to look cool and busy, tripping as you enter. Then, later, he/she gets promoted using your work report.

You spend the next three months (or years) going over in your mind what you could and should and would have said. Over and over you repeat it, refining the words, adjusting your gestures and his/hers, thinking of new angles, feeling the outrage and the indignation, watching him or her squirm. Never done it? Come on!

There are many variations to the loop. You can repeat monologues in response to a politician's new policy, or rehearse your opinion on global warming, you can correct the misconceptions of others on any number of subjects – all totally without opposition!

The loop can work for you, too, as part of the creation of your vision. For many years, in my loop, I was in discussion with Oprah on television. We discussed this very book in fact. At length. She naturally thought it was wonderful, and millions of copies were sold. This is not such a bad loop to be involved in, provided you do not lose sight of reality and all that is to be done there in order to bring that vision into being. This loop is definitely not productive if you don't write the book!

I have no doubt that when I do get to meet Oprah (which I will), somehow, she will remember that we have met before and there will be a sense of *déjà vu*.

The problem with the less constructive type of mental loop is that it hooks your attention and keeps you stuck in an incomplete cycle. It dissipates energy, keeps your mind away from more important things – like making money, in this case – and depending on what your mind keeps regurgitating, it can create and maintain an addiction to negativity. This is not a good thing for anything, and especially not for the creation of a wealth container.

Certainly these blobs of negativity, or self-importance, or in any case 'stuckness', will create big lumpy blocks in your wealth flow.

There are two aspects of hooked attention. On the one hand you need to complete the cycle so that it no longer preys on your mind. On the other hand, you need to lure your mind away from its own grip. Let us start with the first aspect.

8

Hooked Attention – Releasing the Mind

Where is your mind stuck? Where does your money become stuck?

Unfinished Business – Hooked Attention –
Releasing the Mind
Wealth Training Process

A word of caution: Please read again the instructions on how to use this book on pages 252 to 261. If any of the recurring replaying of events in your mind involves trauma of any kind, please do not process that here. Please see a trained professional.

First set your intent on releasing hooked attention in the mind, so that blocks to wealth flow will be released, opening the way to focused attention and increased wealth flow. Do that now, in your own words.

Part One – Ending the Cycle

1. What themes grip your mind in a recurring replay of events? List up to seven items, together with the dominant emotion of each.
2. Create a conclusion for each event. Where possible, adjust physical reality to bring it to a conclusion. For example, confront Mr/s Smug and tell them how you feel in their presence. Take control and set things right.
3. If your mind keeps playing out something you want to tell someone, do it. See them, call them on the telephone or write a letter. Bring the cycle to completion.
4. If an action is needed to complete the cycle, do it, and bring the cycle to conclusion.
5. Keep it simple.
6. If it is impossible to alter reality on the physical, do it in your imagination. Sit in front of the other person in your mind's eye and say what you need to say, or do what you need to do, create a new conclusion and then decide 'it is over'.
7. Perform a symbolic act to imprint on your mind that this cycle is ended. For example, burn the paper on which you wrote the letter, throw a pebble into a river or into the sea for each event you have brought to conclusion.
8. If you are busy lecturing to the world, bring each lecture to a close and say 'it is ended'.
9. As you complete each cycle, tick it off on your list, and imagine the emotion associated with it becoming transformed into golden light which is absorbed into your heart, giving you power and strength.
10. Acknowledge the increased energy and lightness this wealth training has produced.

Releasing the grip

The gripped mind is like a monkey holding on to a handful of nuts inside a jar. The only way he will let go is if you present him with a bunch of bananas. Or, rather, two bunches. Distraction. It works for monkeys, babies, as well as the mind.

You cannot wrench the mind away from something. You cannot force the mind to do anything. You cannot 'not think' of something.

(I absolutely refuse to use the pink elephant example!) You can only gently redirect.

Mental pathways are like physical pathways in the countryside. The more you use them the more they become grooved, the more you habituate to using them. The mind will naturally return to its known pathways – this is called habit. To create a new habit, a new pathway, requires willingness, attention and repetition.

Completing cycles releases trapped energy and clears your energetic flows; it also clears the mind to some extent. It does not obliterate habits, however, and the mind, no matter what symbolic acts you perform, will want to return to its well-known, well-grooved paths. When this happens, remind your mind that this cycle is over and gently direct it to the creation of your wealth container. Give your mind a more interesting challenge to pursue. The mind loves to be busy.

Practise directing your attention on to subjects that you choose. We will draw up a list of these.

Part Two – Redirecting the Mind

1. Create a list of seven fabulous afternoons where time and money are no object.
2. Think of three new hobbies you would like to take up.
3. Describe your ideal home.
4. Create three ideal holidays.
5. Invent three ways to solve global warming.
6. Think of three ways to solve world hunger.
7. What would you do with a million if you had to spend it in a day?

Get yourself a beautiful vase, container or jar. Write up each of your responses to the items above on a separate piece of paper, except for item 7 which you leave as a question. Fold the pieces of paper and put them into your container. Gently redirect the mind by pulling out an item and asking your mind to elaborate on it. You can also create your own prompts.

> *Imagine the power of our actions if each one*
> *contained one hundred percent of our attention*
> Thich Nhat Hanh from The Art of Power

Unfinished business – mental congestion

We live in a fast world, full of stimulus. We are bombarded with information, movement, energetic waves of every kind. We can no longer focus on just one thing – while working on the computer, an email arrives, the phone rings and an sms creeps in too. We rush around in our fast cars, eating fast food, quickly, while listening to the news. Congestion and indigestion is the result.

Slow down. Breathe. Stop. Listen. Meditate. Relax. Take a walk in the countryside. Go for a week without television or the news – even if you are an investment broker – read only the business papers. Do a three-day mental detox. Take ten minutes each day to relax – in silence.

To direct wealth to your container requires focused intent. To have focused intent you need your attention in the present. Release the mind from hooked attention by completing cycles and directing it along the cultivation of useful pathways. Clear mental congestion through relaxation and silence.

Meditation is a very useful tool for creating space in the mind. Meditation can be done in many forms. There is the traditional sitting quietly and allowing what thoughts arise to arise. There is walking meditation where you walk slowly, with attention. Any activity when done fully in the present, with attention, can become a form of meditation. So consider gardening, sailing, swimming, taking tea as a way of creating a haven of space in your life. It does not matter what you do, what matters is the spirit in which you do it.

There is the story of the student seeking the way to meditation and inner stillness.

'Master, where shall I begin?' he asked.

The Master held up a finger. 'Shhh,' he said. 'Can you hear the roar of that waterfall?'

The student listened intently. 'Yes, I can,' he answered after a while.

'Begin there,' said the Master.

After a while the student asked, 'What if I was unable to hear the waterfall, Master? What would you have said then?'

The Master held up a finger. 'I would have told you to begin there,' he answered.

Start where you are.

> *Many small makes a great*
> Geoffrey Chaucer

9

Unexecuted Intentions

What things have been left unsaid? What things have been left undone?

Unfinished business – unexecuted intentions – what is left undone or unsaid

When it became clear that my mother who was in hospital in a coma was not going to recover, I was filled with guilt and remorse. There was so much I wished I had said and done. I scanned all the years of coldness and disdain towards her. I thought back on her early days in hospital and how unsupportive I had been. I even remembered when she'd first shown me the dark bruise on her leg which had developed into the cancer. She'd said, 'Look at this on my leg, isn't it strange, what do you think it is?'

I had barely glanced at it, shrugged and mumbled, 'I don't know.'

Now she was dying, and all the years of abuse in my childhood seemed to melt in the face of this woman, my stepmother, whom I had only recently come to forgive and love. But I had never told her.

And so I sat alone, with my eyes closed, for one night and then for two and three and I called her up in my mind's eye and I told her everything I had wanted to say. She told me many things too, how she was sorry, what lessons she had taught me, and how she loved me. I wept at the impending loss of my mother.

By the time she died, I was at peace. Nothing was left unsaid, even though we never once said anything to one another in the physical world, as she never came out of her coma.

It is not the things we do or say, but the things left unsaid and undone that affect us the most. Some people spend a lifetime wishing they had said goodbye, or sorry, or I love you. Others wish they had taken that trip, or done that course, or taken that risk. Unexecuted intentions create boulders that redirect the flow of our wealth totally away from our container, blocking it and stopping the flow.

I am so incredibly thankful that I had the opportunity and good sense to end the cycle with my mother in the way I did. Had I not done so, I am sure the guilt would have grown immense by now, poisoning my system and keeping many good things away.

What we leave unsaid and undone can become a festering wound that eventually cripples us. But let's lighten up a bit! It need not be so. We can change things, right now, today. Let's do that now.

Unexecuted Intentions
Wealth Training Process

Write without thinking. Allow what emerges to emerge. What may come up as important may not be what you would normally think of as important. Trust the process.

1. List up to seven things you have left unsaid. What emotion arises with each item? Circle it.
2. List up to seven things you have left undone. Circle the emotion for each.

3. If today was your last day on earth, what would you wish you had done that you did not?
4. If today was your last day on earth, what would you wish you had done differently?
5. If today was your last day on earth, what do you wish you had said?
6. If you could blow caution to the wind, what would you want to finish?

Inspired Action

1. Take inspired action!
2. List any decisions you have taken and any actions you wish to perform. Do them.
3. Item by item, complete these cycles. Start with the easy and simple ones.
4. Say what was left unsaid. Do what was left undone. Blow caution to the wind. Do it!
5. Bring each cycle to completion.
6. If people are no longer around, have the conversation in your mind's eye or write a letter, or do the action in your mind's eye if physical completion is impossible.

Note: When doing things in your mind's eye you may need to do them many times until you feel a sense of completion. Do not rush or give up too soon. Repeat as many times as needed until you feel the cycle is complete.

7. As you complete each cycle, tick it off on your list, and imagine the emotion associated with it becoming transformed into golden light which is absorbed into your heart.
8. Acknowledge the increased energy and lightness this wealth training has produced.
9. Rejoice!

Five, four, three, two, bungee!
A story

I must tell you about my bungee jump. Many, many moons ago, before Shaun and I were married, we were travelling along the Garden Route and stopped to look over the Bloukrans River bridge

– third largest in the world – near the no stopping sign . . . Lo and behold, a girl with a radiant face was being pulled up on a rope. She said, 'Wow, that was the most amazing thing I have ever done!'

At 210 metres, it was indeed 'the biggest bungee jump in the world by far', just like the T-shirt said, and it had been erected a mere five days before. Shaun had always wanted to bungee and I, lured by the girl's enthusiasm, wanted to experience what it must surely feel like to fly. So off we went.

Walking across a metal bridge in the howling wind some 250 metres above a gorge and river, it started to get scary. At the end of the walkway, people from around the world – adventurers, coaches, adrenaline junkies, and thrill-seekers – huddled around a large earthenware sandpit puffing on cigarettes to the sound of thumping music. No matter the background, no matter how many times they had bungeed before, no matter how many other life-threatening thrills they had undertaken, everyone standing on the edge of that bridge before jumping that day felt absolutely and totally terrified – even those who had dived with sharks.

So there I was on Bloukrans Bridge hobbling to the edge between the arms of two chunky New Zealanders, my feet tied together with rope, the music thumping. At the very edge I looked down. You can't help it, especially because they tell you not to (it's that pink elephant thing). At that moment my body, my mind, every fibre of my being screamed, 'NO! No, death, no!'

The music is thumping, the wind is howling and they say, 'We'll start the countdown and when we get to zero, you just let go of our arms.'

'No, death, no,' my body says.

I say no, I can't do this. They say let's just start the countdown. I know if they do, they'll let go of me and I'll be over that edge. No, I say, I can't do this, and slowly we hobble away from the edge.

They told me I could jump later, or come back the next day, it was up to me. They were very kind, those men, and highly experienced in the psychology of facing death.

So I sat on a chair in the freezing howling wind, shaking uncontrollably from head to toe and I watched as one by one everyone jumped. I did not know what I was going to do. I knew that if I left I would not be coming back. Eventually, I decided that no matter what happened when I jumped that day, it could not possibly be worse than the feeling I would be left with if I did not jump at all. I simply could not leave this cycle unfinished.

So, right at the very end, with anxiety gripping my stomach, frozen with cold, and still shaking from head to toe – 'I'm cold,' I told the New Zealand bungee coach. 'No, honey,' he said, 'you're just scared' – I hobbled to the edge once more, ignored my terrified body, and shut my eyes and jumped!

Whoosh! I was sucked into a whirlpool of wind; loud, howling wind. I spun around a few times and then began to fall into the arms of silence. Deep, deep stillness; there was not a sound when slowly and clearly a smile emerged, chased by bubbles of thrill, tumbling out as a river of extreme exhilaration at the joy of being alive! I am alive, I am alive, this is amazing! Down, down, down I sank as my spirits soared. At the bottom after a few rebounds I hung upside down in a verdant valley, gazing at the river and the sea beyond, feeling completely enlivened and totally centred.

When I was pulled up, my face reflected the face of the girl whose radiance had lured me into this adventure. For me, bungee jumping was about a near death experience, overcoming fear of mortality, transcending fear of death. It was about connecting with elation and expansiveness and going beyond limits.

I would never have had this experience if I had walked away. I would never have known the thrill of flight if I had left this cycle incomplete. So now on my death bed I will not have to worry about not completing that bungee jump! Phew! What a relief! One less thing to worry about . . .

Remembering my bungee jump reminds me of a poem I wrote in my women's writing class – way, way, *way* before I had so much as written the first word of the first draft of *Money Alchemy*. But I *did* know I was going to write a book!

Jump off the edge!
A poem

I'm going to jump off the edge,
leap up from my bed!

Out of the car, out of the blues,
I'm going to kick mediocrity,
with high heeled shoes
I'm going to give the finger
to do's and shoulds
and even possibilities,
'cause they don't rhyme
I'm going to jump up, leap off, shake out, fly, and climb!

I'm going to write up a storm,
then do it again
I'm going to sing out bestsellers
and walk in the rain with
an umbrella of starlight, and nothing else

I'm going to kick timidity in the butt
or maybe its arse,
'cause it doesn't rhyme
and you can't keep a good thing down –
that would be a crime

Believing in magic!
Fire!
Jump the edge!
Fly into tomorrow and

peer over the ledge
to see yourself climbing
out of your book
have a peek, have a peek,
have another look

I'm going to stretch out my wings
and write that book.
Look!

(und I did . . .)

Rise to the challenge

We leave things incomplete because there is some kind of stressful element attached to completing the action. There is fear, or an emotion we do not want to experience. Be aware of and acknowledge this fact. See overcoming such a challenge as a kind of vision quest which, when successfully completed, will not only clear huge blocks in your wealth flow but will also cultivate courage and faith, expanding limitations and raising the ceiling of what is possible! Five, four, three, two, Bungee! Go for it!

We have dealt with unfinished business on the physical and mental levels. In the next section on 'Relationships' we will cover unfinished business on the emotional level, always bearing in mind that the distinction between mental, physical and emotional is not black and white and is made here for ease of reference only.

. . . You cannot see outside of you what you fail to see inside
Anthony de Mello from *One Minute Wisdom*

10

Relationships – Adding Value to Life

Which relationships drain your energy and wealth flow?
Which relationships add value?

Relationships

Probably a subject for a whole book on its own, there can be no doubt in anybody's mind that relationships are a major source of leaks and blocks which restrict the flow of money to our wealth container.

And it's not just your mean boss or the taxman who is the problem. It's not just that tight-fisted husband with no idea of the cost of good lingerie. No, the problem is a lot bigger than that in the arena of relationships, and it affects everyone.

The solution, however, is very simple. And if you are someone who likes to get to the point quickly, you can skip this whole section and simply answer the following two questions. These questions can be used to assess not only the value of your relationship to anyone or to anything, they can also be used as a basis for any type of decision making. The questions are:

1. Does (or will) .... (insert name of person, or thing, or decision) add value?
2. Does (or will) .... (insert name of person, or thing, or decision) expand or contract my world?

What does value mean? You decide. But if the person you are in relationship with does not add value and does not expand your world you need to ask yourself what is the purpose of that relationship. In *The Prophet* Khalil Gibran says 'Let there be no purpose in friendship other than the deepening of Spirit'. That refers to an expansion, without a doubt. So we are not only talking plain materialism here.

We become confused about the value of relationships because of the notion of 'unconditional love'. And, let's face it, who doesn't want a 'no questions asked over the lingerie bill' policy? It's only human to *expect* unconditional devotion from everyone you meet, but to *give* it? Now that's another question . . .

Frivolity aside, though, when, as a result of any relationship, your world, or any part of it, is contracting, when, as a result of any relationship you are losing value – of self, possessions, joy, dignity, pride, respect, creativity, potential – then you cannot cite unconditional love as the culprit. You cannot say, 'I put up with this because of unconditional love.' No.

If you are losing value, or contracting in a relationship, and all your best efforts to change this have not succeeded, it's best to replace that relationship with some nice dark chocolate, a good bottle of wine, or someone more able to deliver continuous unconditional devotion like say a dog, *tout de suite* and pronto! This is good advice. It doesn't matter what you are doing to attract the situation (if this is your thinking). First abandon the sinking ship before you drown, then you can see a therapist and figure it all out. Let me first mention, though, that this advice is not merely for men and women in love; it is good advice for business, investment decisions, selection of staff or business partners – even your choice of lingerie. Try it, and you'll see. It makes all decision making quite simple.

Back to the matter at hand, moneymaking, containing money, and blocks and leaks in money flow caused by relationships and, specifically, unfinished emotional business in relationships.

Unfinished business on the emotional level can have very serious repercussions on moneymaking. Generally speaking, it will cause huge leaks in both your piping and your container. This means that money energy coming your way will dissipate and leak away. It will never reach its destination. Suppressed emotions, like compressed steam, will, over time, damage and eventually blow up whatever they are contained in. Unreleased grief slowly drips away, decreasing vital life force. And incomplete actions, things we wish we had or hadn't done, have the effect of immobilising us, freezing the flow of energy and wealth streaming towards us.

We will look at relationships past and present from two perspectives – the perspective of self and the perspective of others. In other words, we will look at unfinished business where 'they' are responsible, and unfinished business where we are responsible. Naturally, we know it's all 'their' fault – that is a given . . . However, we will try to release and redirect all the precious energy tied up with this unfinished business so that we can use it to enhance our wealth (and that will show them!).

Relationships exist on many levels – there is relationship to self, to significant others and to family, to groups, to nations, all the way to our relationship to the universe. For the purposes of what we are doing, we will look at our relationship to self and to the Divine, and to others in general.

We will examine our unfinished business as a two-way cycle, looking at our part and the part of others in these cycles.

But do they make you feel like dancing?

There is a very simple way to know whether or not someone is adding value to your life. How do you feel in their presence and, more importantly, how do you feel after you have left them? If you feel down, depressed, uncomfortable, less than, deflated, unin-

214

spired, if there is a little knot of anxiety in your stomach, if the world looks a little less rosy than it did before, if your great plan to make a fortune does not look so great any more (never mind if they know better), if you are feeling more serious and adult and responsible, and if this is more or less how this person or group always makes you feel – THEN DITCH THIS RELATIONSHIP PRONTO! Yes, I know I've said this before – this is for emphasis!

It does not matter if you have known them for twenty years, or if you are related to them or if they are the members of your golf club. If someone is shrinking your world on a constant basis, disconnect. If someone is draining or taking away your energy on a constant basis, this is not of benefit to you.

Now I know that there are schools of thought that say accept your current situation and it will change. There are approaches that say look and see what you are doing to create this in your life and change that. And there are others who say you have exactly what you need in your life right now for your growth.

All of these approaches are true and there is a time and place for them all. There is also a predisposition for them all. Some work for some people and some for others. Nothing is absolute.

What I am saying is that for the purposes of repairing energetic leaks and blocks in the flow of your wealth, I suggest you disconnect from those who routinely drain you of your energy, enthusiasm and hope. I believe this is good advice.

You want to surround yourself with people who inspire you, make you feel lighter about the world, give you hope, make you laugh, encourage you to chase your dreams and help you to do so. You want to be around people who help you to expand. And if just reading about it gives you a lift, imagine what it would do for you in real life?

Let me tell you a little secret. Once you have let go of someone in a relationship in your heart and mind, they actually just go away of their own accord. You don't have to 'break up' or do or say anything, it happens naturally on its own. Here is a process that shows you how.

Letting Go of Sulky Sarah (or maybe it's Sam)
Wealth Training Process

First set your intent on releasing blocks and repairing leaks in your wealth flow through releasing those who would drain your energy, with love and good wishes. Do this now, in your own words.

1. Without thinking too hard, write a list of all the people and groups that shrink you as a being to a limit of seven. If you cannot think of any, ask yourself who drains you? Who makes you feel small or stupid? Who makes you feel less of yourself? Who leaves you with anxiety in your stomach? Who makes you feel you should grow up and face the world and become more serious? They are the ones.
2. Next to each item, write the emotion/s that they elicit in you and circle the emotion/s.
3. Take (up to) seven pieces of paper and do the following for each person. You may wish to deal with only one person at a time, depending on how powerful an effect they have on you.
    (a) draw a border around the edge of the paper
    (b) write the person's name at the top
    (c) inside the border write everything that comes to mind about that person and how they make you feel. Write for three minutes
    (d) when you are finished, turn the page over and write the the person a farewell letter for three minutes. This can take any form, and you may use any language you like. Thank the person for your past association and any good they have done for you
    (e) When you are done, write 'I release and let go of .... (name), and .... (name) releases me. May you go in peace'
4. When you are done writing, sit quietly and in your mind's eye see the person you have been writing about quietly leave your life. Say your goodbyes. Wish them well for the future.
5. As the person leaves, imagine the emotions associated with that person transformed into golden light in your heart. The golden light radiates throughout your body and beyond opening up the flows of wealth, and releasing any blocks.
6. Set your intent to end this cycle.
7. Burn the paper in an appropriate manner, and say 'it is done'.

Inspired Action

1. Take inspired action!
2. List any decisions you have taken and any actions you wish to perform. Do them.
3. Think of three new people who inspire you and begin to cultivate relationships with these people.
4. Acknowledge the increased energy and lightness this wealth training has produced.
5. Rejoice!

We are bubbles of energy
Carlos Castaneda from *The Fire from Within*

11

Relationships – Transforming Regret: Right Action

What do you wish you'd never done or said?

Transforming regret

When we hurt others, we hurt ourselves. That is universal law, because everything is connected. When we hurt, we are not in the present. When we are not in the present we are not standing in our power. When we are not standing in our power we cannot create the wealth we need or, indeed, see it even when it is all around us. When we are hurt we shrink, we become less of who we are.

Many of the things we have done to others may have been done in a moment of anger, or foolishness, while under the influence of something or other, or at a time when we felt very differently from how we feel now. We may regret doing some of these things, and it is this regret which creates unfinished business in the emotional arena. Because on some level, we wish it had been different. We wish we'd said this or that, we wish we'd done something different. Often we simply wish we could say sorry. In other words, we wish for a different ending. And while we wish for a different ending, it's not ended, is it?

Regret is a terrible burden. It closes the heart and pushes the world away. Regret de-magnetises the flow of wealth, pushing it away from us. Because when we feel regret, we feel we are not good enough, not worthy. And if we do not feel worthy, how can we increase our wealth? If we do not feel worthy, how can wealth come to us?

A very important thing here is not to replace regret with guilt. This is crucial. What we are doing is tying up unfinished business in the area of relationships so as to release energy and repair leaks in our wealth flow and container.

Things you wish you'd never done (or said)

Okay, so we've all had one of *those* nights when we wake up the next day and think, 'Oh my. . . !'

And everyone is entitled to a few of those in every lifetime – okay, let's make that every decade.

What we are talking about here, though, is something hurtful, unfair, unjust, or just plain nasty that you may have done to someone that *in your opinion* was really not something you should have done or said. I stress the words *in your opinion*, because this is all about you, and how you feel. If you were plain downright rude but have no stressed feelings about it, even though everyone you know thinks your behaviour was outrageous, then that item should not be on this list. Not unless you constantly replay the event in your mind, in which case you may wish to process it under the previous section.

We are looking at things you have done or said which you regret, and where this regret is sitting as a blob of stuck emotion, which is stuck energy, somewhere deep inside of you. This stuck energy is disrupting the general flow of energy in your life, and it is also disrupting the flow of wealth towards you.

Any and all stuck emotion is like a blob or glob in a pipe. Yucky, mucky, and something we avoid looking at. Imagine a fur ball, hairball, or lump of dirty lard blocking up your drains. This is the emotional equivalent here. We all collect fur balls which we need to cough up. Unexpressed emotion, emotion connected with things we wish we had or had not done, covert feelings about people; in short, not being true to what we feel, is a source of a lot of disease and discomfort in our lives. We need to clear these emotions out. Let them go. Cough them up. We need to clear the flows in our lives and in so doing, release the energy flow of wealth towards us.

Research shows that it's the things we wish we'd done and did not, that actually hold the most emotion. And we will deal with that in the next section. But let's start with the easy things first. Things we wish we'd never done (or said).

Cough up those emotional fur balls

Now, perhaps the person we hissed at is long gone (and who could blame them?). Perhaps we do not know where they are, or how to reach them. Perhaps they are no longer even alive. This does not matter. It is obviously first prize to deal directly with the person, if you can find them.

A big part of ending these emotional cycles is taking your power back. There is enormous power in being able to say 'I'm sorry' – no matter what Ryan O'Neal said in that 'Love Story' movie. There is an enormous wealth of energy that becomes stuck every time we have done someone else harm and we feel bad about it.

Feeling bad and, worse still, feeling guilty is an energy drain similar to a sucking vortex. All goodness flowing towards you just fades away. Feeling bad diminishes who you are, how you think of yourself, how you feel about yourself, and ultimately you project this into the outside world where others pick up on it, and reflect the same back to you.

You simply cannot hope to attract wealth while you run around thinking very little of yourself because you are so stuck in guilt and feeling bad. Now, the biggest culprits of energy drain in the 'feeling bad' department are not those big, momentous events. We can usually laugh those off, or convince ourselves that it was the other fellow's fault, and become very self righteous and indignant. The biggest culprits are those iffy, knot-in-the-stomach, not-quite-sure-if-he-took-offence, is-it-really-how-I-see-it situations.

When you don't know why you're avoiding him

Let me give you some examples. You are standing in the queue at the check-out counter and someone tries to cut in. You are feeling tetchy because (do you need a reason?) it's raining and you spent ages trying to find parking. You bite the person's head off and they cringe and skulk back to the end of the queue. You may regret doing that later, you may wish you had been more diplomatic. And, indeed, you may wish to apologise to that person in this exercise. That is one pretty clear example of something done that you may wish you hadn't, and you're clear about what happened.

What we are hoping to get to, though, once we are through all the obvious examples like the one above, is something like this. John is the one in your social group who is always teased. He is a real sport about it and laughs like everyone else. One day you let slip that he fancies one of the girls (or guys) in the group, which you know no one else suspected. Apart from a single moment when a wounded look crosses his eyes, he gives no other sign that your revelation is a problem. Everyone laughs about it, and so does he. But that moment's wounded look plays back in your mind, and it is linked to a sinking feeling in your stomach. And as a result (though you cite work, no time, and a new lover as the excuse), you stop hanging around with 'the guys' as much as you used to, and when you next spot John in the distance in the shopping centre, you quickly duck into a shop.

Now *that* is unresolved emotion around something you wish you hadn't done, which (though apparently far more innocuous) is far more damaging to you emotionally than the first example as it is buried away from consciousness where it can grow and fester. You may need some pretty open and honest reflection to uncover such events. Once you call John and apologise, you will generally find that the relief you feel will far surpass any emotion John may still have about this – depending of course on how long ago the event took place (and the exact nature of what you said or did – obviously, if everyone else thought John was one of the lads, he may still have pretty strong feelings about your revelation if, for example, it was one of the guys that he fancied).

We have all experienced similar situations in life – situations where we cannot pinpoint an event yet we seem to have, inexplicably, 'fallen out' with someone, or we have a sudden urge to avoid them. There is a certain something in the air which we cannot define, and we are uncomfortable, even anxious, around this other person who, not so long ago, may have been our bosom-buddy. We cannot put our finger on it. We are unsure what happened. All we know is that something is not right, and we feel bad.

To unearth such events, we will use a special process of focusing on people whose presence makes us uncomfortable. But first, let's start with the obvious.

Things you wish you'd never done (or said): The Obvious Suspects
Wealth Training Process

Do the following with compassion and without judgement. Set the clear intent of releasing energy blocks in your money flow caused by stuck emotions in the area of relationships.

1. Without thinking too hard, list all the things you wish you'd never done or said to a limit of seven, as they arise in your mind.
2. Next to each item, write the emotion/s that the event elicits in you then and now, and circle the emotion/s.
3. For each person, do the following. Deal with only one person at a time, and depending on how strongly you feel about the incident, resolving one person per day should be enough.
    (a) In your mind's eye, apologise to the person, and say anything you wish to say to them. Saying it out loud is best. Find a quiet place where you will be undisturbed or do it in your car when you are in traffic.
    (b) In your mind's eye, replay the event and change it, to reach a more harmonious conclusion.
    (c) In your mind's eye, see the energy in the emotions around this

event, both past and present, transform into golden light in your heart and radiate throughout your body and into the world beyond. This golden light dissolves any blocks in your wealth flow and in your life and attracts all good things to you.

(d) Affirm to yourself and to the world that this is so.

(e) If you know where the person is, call them and apologise, or go and see them, and say anything you need to say to them about this event. You may write a letter or email only if you absolutely cannot find a telephone number.

(f) If the person is no longer alive, or you have no idea how to reach them, then doing it in your mind's eye as above is sufficient, or you may want to write a letter too.

(g) Once you have spoken or written to the person, again transform the energy as in (c) and (d) above.

(h) When you are finished, wash your hands, burn the letter (if the person is unreachable), and say 'it is done'.

(i) Now take the time to forgive yourself. See yourself (or your concept of the Divine) cradling you as child or infant. Wrap yourself in the arms of unconditional love, and tell yourself it's okay. It's okay to make mistakes, it's okay to mess up. Tell yourself you are loved, no matter what you have done. Allow whatever emotions arise to emerge and flow. See these emotions as releasing the energy flow of your wealth and life. This is a very important step. Take as much time as you need. Do not rush it. You may wish to write yourself a letter of forgiveness.

(j) Perform a symbolic act of completion. You may wish to dance a dance of release; or drink a shot of something, throwing the glass behind your shoulder, Russian style (the breaking of glass is regarded as a shattering of negative energy); or maybe simply wash your hands. Let yourself off the hook.

(k) Decide this cycle is finished. Say it out loud and clap your hands three times. Why? It's more fun!

Things you wish you'd never done (or said): The Strange and the Squirmy
Wealth Training Process

Do the following with compassion and without judgement. Set the clear intent of releasing energy blocks in your money flow caused by stuck emotions in the area of relationships.

1. List all the people you have been avoiding lately, people who make you feel uncomfortable, or angry, or cause a knot to form in your stomach when you see them, or where there is a strange energy and you feel it's because of something you've done.
2. Sit in a quiet space, and set your intent on seeing the root of the problem with compassion and without judgement.
3. Think back to the last time you saw the person who makes you feel uncomfortable, and then the time before that, and before that, and so on, until you get to a time when things between you were good and there were no uncomfortable feelings.
4. Then go forward, one event at a time until you find 'the one' that changed things. Sometimes your intuition will take you straight to the event. Allow this to happen.
5. Replay what happened and watch as a neutral observer.
6. Discover what it is that you said or did to upset the energetic balance between you and this person. This may simply be a hunch or a feeling – go with it.
7. Allow the other person's perspective to emerge without judgement. If you think calling their dog smelly is a silly reason for them to get all hurt and offended, it does not matter. What matters is to find the thing that you said or did that has created a rift between you and to acknowledge your part in causing someone else emotional discomfort, even if you do not understand it or agree with it.
8. Where appropriate, or if you are completely flummoxed, you may wish to see or call the other person and simply ask them what happened in their opinion.
9. Sometimes 'what happened' will reveal itself as a certain feeling or impression that you may have, that you cannot prove or know for sure. Go with it.
10. Once you have discovered the event, proceed as in the previous Wealth Training Process (The Obvious Suspects) above.

On the path of knowledge, nothing is as clear as we'd like
it to be
Carlos Castaneda

12

Relationships – Transforming Regret: Right Thinking

What do you wish you'd never thought?

Things you wish you'd never thought

Sometimes we think really nasty things about others, often in rage or in a moment of thoughtlessness. We know that thoughts have power. We know that everything is energy. We know that everything is connected; and that if you think something, it can, depending on the depth of emotion behind that thought, bring that something into being. Even if what we thought about another did not come into being, sending negative energy towards someone will affect them. They will feel the negativity on some level, and we will too.

Therefore, we need to be aware of what we think. We need to

direct our thinking skilfully and compassionately. And when it comes to others we need to direct thoughts towards them that will be of benefit, thoughts that will nourish and enrich their lives. And as we enrich and nourish others, so we too become enriched and nourished. That's just the way things work.

As a young child, I read somewhere that there was little difference between thinking of murdering someone and actually doing it. This had a profound effect on my thinking, and was probably one of the foundation blocks for my understanding of energy. I read that one should not go to bed with 'anger towards one's brother'. And so, for my entire life as a child, and later as a teenager, I faithfully wiped the slate of the day clean every evening before going to bed. I forgave and let go (to the best of my ability) so that I would not go to bed with anger towards my brother in my heart. This was truly excellent advice, and a fabulous practice which I would recommend to everyone. To this day, I try to wipe the slate clean. Perhaps not as religiously as I did in childhood, but certainly this is a part of my practice.

The point is, thoughts can harm. It is good to retract and cancel a careless thought as soon as we become aware of it. We do this simply by saying just that. On the other hand, it is also important not to blame ourselves, or spend years in guilt over things that in all likelihood had little to do with us. Sometimes, especially as children, we think an unkind thought and then suddenly that person is ill or maybe even dead and we blame ourselves. This is not useful at all.

We will now process around this subject. If believing that your thinking can affect someone is not part of your reality at this time, then skip this exercise. It's better to remain true to yourself than to pretend. You'll still get to heaven, I promise . . .

Right thinking: Things you wish you'd never thought
Advanced Wealth Transformation

Please read through instructions before you begin. Allow at least an hour of uninterrupted time. This exercise requires clear focus. Do it when you feel refreshed and once you have already completed a fair amount of the processing in this book.

Please take careful note of the warning on processing under 'The Basics'.

Do the following with compassion and without judgement. Set the clear intent of releasing energy blocks in your money flow caused by stuck emotions in the area of relationships.

1. Ask for the protection of the Divine as you do this processing.
2. Imagine a wall of protection around you which keeps all the emotions and energy you are dealing with here safely within the realms of Transformational Wealth Processing.
3. Create an imaginary circle within which the Transformational Wealth Processing will take place.
4. Now make a large circle on a big piece of paper – A4 or A3 size.
5. Make a list of people about whom you routinely entertain unkind or even vicious thoughts within the circle.
6. Become aware of the energy linked to each thought. Write this down next to each item.
7. Become aware of the energy and thoughts coming back at you from this person. Record this too.
8. Imagine a fire burning brightly before you. Add fuel and sweet smelling oils to it.
9. Picture yourself throwing each unkind thought and its associated emotions into this fire.
10. Picture the thoughts, emotions and energy the other person is sending towards you also going into the fire.
11. The colour of this unskilful thought energy is a dark grey.
12. As the unskilful thought and emotion burns, the flame transforms the grey energy into a column of golden light. Allow all the grey energy to transform to gold before you stop, no matter how long this takes.
13. Now absorb the golden light energy into yourself through your heart and feel it spread throughout your body and mind.
14. The golden light fills you with positive good energy and flows out from you into the world attracting all good things to you, and clearing your wealth flow.
15. The golden light energy flows to the other person too, bringing them luck and good fortune.

17. When you are finished watch as the fire dies down and is gone.
18. Take the paper with the unkind thoughts on it and cross each one out.
19. As you cross the thoughts out, state your intent that these unskilful thoughts are cancelled.
20. Burn the paper in an appropriate way when you are done.
21. Wash your hands.
22. Say 'it is done'.
23. Create three new positive thoughts for each person. You can send the same three thoughts to each one if you like.
24. Send the thoughts out with all the good energy you can muster, and imagine them winging their way towards their destination.
25. Absorb the good feelings that this process has initiated.
26. Decide to monitor your thoughts and undertake to transform any unskilful thinking as soon as you become aware of it.
27. Rejoice and celebrate!
28. Acknowledge that this process has opened up your wealth flows and cleared energetic debris from your life.
29. This is powerful processing. Take a break for a few days.
30. Prepare to receive.

Here is a tale I wrote, especially for you.

The little boy and the grey donkey
A tale

Once upon a time, in a land far, far away, there was a young boy who lived alone in a village. His parents were both dead and he had no one in the world except a little grey donkey. They lived together in an abandoned hut at the edge of the forest.

The boy and the donkey worked in the village, fetching and carrying and running errands. In this way he eked out a meagre existence which, together with the roots and nuts he foraged, kept him and the donkey alive. The boy always made certain that the donkey was the first to eat. He rubbed him down with a brush of straw and once a week he would find or buy an apple or a carrot. This treat always made the donkey bray in delight, kicking up his hind feet in a little dance.

Every night, before he went to bed, the little boy said his prayers as his mother had taught him. He gave thanks for his food and shelter and he thanked each person that he'd met that day, sending them good wishes for their health and well-being. For his mother had said, whatever thoughts you send out to others will be multiplied tenfold and return to you. 'So be aware, my boy, of what you think of others,' his mother had said. 'And think naught that would cause any harm.'

Now, late one winter's day, a stranger came to the village. He was a big, burly man, bearded and strong. He had a large cart driven by two handsome donkeys. He set up shop at the centre of the village hiring out his services and that of his cart and donkeys to fetch and cart and carry.

Because of his size and superior strength, because of the power of his cart and donkeys, he made light work of all the tasks the villagers entrusted to him, and the little boy and his donkey were slowly forgotten. No one asked the little boy to fetch wood or carry milk any longer and, as the dark of winter approached, the little boy found himself cold and hungry in his hut at the edge of the wood.

As the cold set in, the little boy huddled next to the donkey and, despite what his mother had taught him, he wished with all his might that the big, burly man would fall down a cliff and disappear. He imagined all sorts of things happening to the big burly man, none of them pleasant, all of them different, except for the ending which was always the same. In the end, the people would go back to using the little boy and his grey donkey to fetch and cart and carry. The little boy would be warm and fed once more.

The more the little boy thought in this way, the angrier he felt, and the grimmer his life appeared. One night, when he was so hungry he could hear his tummy rumble, his mother came to him in a dream.

'Whatever you think of others will be multiplied tenfold,' she said. Over and over again she repeated this advice until the little boy woke up with the words ringing so clearly in his ears he half expected to find his mother sitting in the hut with him.

He spent the whole morning thinking these words over. 'Whatever you think of others will be multiplied tenfold,' she had said.

What should he think of others? What should he try to multiply tenfold that would change his fortune? And how could he do this while causing none to be harmed?

Over and over the little boy pondered these questions while his tummy rumbled and the winter winds howled.

Eventually, as the light of day began to wane, he had the answer. He shut his eyes tight, ignored the ache in his empty tummy, and began to form a new picture in his mind. In it he saw the big burly man prospering – it was hard at first, but the more he formed the picture, the easier it became. He saw the big burly man becoming busier and busier, growing his business and expanding beyond the boundaries of the village. For seven days and seven nights the little boy, ignoring the howling winds and his increasingly waning life force, sent out his thoughts for a prosperous life for the big burly man.

Now, on the morning of the eighth day, when the little boy and his grey donkey had almost passed out from cold and hunger, there came the muffled sound of hoofs on the snow. The little boy watched as if in a dream as the big burly man made a fire, all the while stuffing into his mouth as much as he could fit of the freshly baked bread he'd been given. He watched as the man fed and watered the grey donkey too, before he sat down next to the now crackling fire and lit a pipe of sweet smelling tobacco. 'That's better,' the man said. 'We can't have my new partners freezing to death now, can we?'

To this day, nobody but the little boy knows how it came to pass that on a cold winter's day the big burly man took the little orphan boy and his grey donkey into his home. Some speculate that he may be the boy's father. Why else would he practically hand over a thriving business to the boy, while he moves on to greener pastures?

And to this day the little boy, who is now a grown man with children of his own, gives thanks at the end of each day, and sends thoughts of prosperity and well-being to everyone he meets. And when he is asked for the secret of his success, he says without a moment's hesitation, 'Whatever you think of others, will be multiplied tenfold.'

> *Two things make a story. The net*
> *and the air that falls through the net.*
> Pablo Neruda

13

Relationships – Transforming Regret: Creating New Pathways

What do you wish you'd done or said?

Things you wish you'd done

Just to reorientate a little, we are looking at unfinished business in the emotional arena, and how this impacts on blocking our wealth flow. We are still working with the image of a container for our wealth and looking at money as unformed, un-manifest energy, flowing towards this wealth container along an underground pipe. In fact, it is a river which we contain and direct along a pipe. The pipe is created by our attention and our intention.

Emotions are energy. Stuck, unresolved emotions create energetic lumps and blocks in our money flow, and may even cause the flow to redirect completely, moving away from our container in a totally different direction. We cannot understand this when it happens. We are doing everything right, we have our budgets in place, we balance our cheque book, earn more than we spend, and follow all the good advice on proper wealth creation and positive living, and still we seem to move slowly away from our goal. Still we do not make money.

The culprit is more often than not some unresolved lump of emotion not only blocking, but redirecting the energetic flow of wealth in our lives. The good news is that it is much easier to fix this than to pass a camel through the eye of a needle.

Probably the most emotion tied up with unfinished business in the emotional arena, is in the area of things we wish we'd done.

That little word 'regret', when you really think about it, is seldom used in the context of what has been done already. It's always those things wished for, longed for, yearned for, that we leave undone, that we regret. And again it may not be the big 'wish I'd become a rock star' stuff that we regret. It's things like not accepting that kiss (remember the whole of the movie 'First Knight' revolves around just that), or not giving that poor child a meal, or not going off on that Cape to Cairo trip, or not finishing the climb up Kilimanjaro.

These are the things we hear people reminiscing about on their death beds.

Here is a quick process, which will bypass all the blah blah.

Things you wish you'd done (or said): The Possible
Wealth Training Process

1. Imagine you are on your death bed, right now. Think back on your life and list all the things you wish you'd done. Write for three minutes.
2. Underline important words and phrases with a different coloured pen.
3. Extract a numbered list from the above, of all the things you wish you'd done.
4. Remove any items which may no longer seem important – emotionally important, that is.

5. Write up a new list of all the things that you still wish you'd done – those things with the greatest emotional charge.
6. Next to each item, write the emotion associated with it and circle it in a different coloured pen.
7. Now go through the list and mark the three most important ones.
8. Go out there and DO what you wanted to do! SAY what you wanted to say! Make it right. Complete the cycle!
9. Rejoice!
10. Acknowledge the release of energetic blocks in your money flow that this process has enabled.
11. Acknowledge the increased lightness and joy this process has created in you.
12. Prepare to receive all good things coming to you!

Okay, let's get a (little) bit realistic. (S)He may no longer be young and beautiful and, besides, (s)he's now married and so are you. Cape to Cairo may no longer be as feasible as it was thirty years ago, and if you couldn't face Kilimanjaro in your twenties you certainly may not want to face it now. So how do we complete and let go? Or, as they say in the American classics, how do we 'get closure'?

Well, fortunately we have available to us this little thing called *alchemy*. The important thing here is that we release the stuck emotion; that is the key. While it would obviously be nice if we could get to do all the things we wish we'd done, that is not always possible. What we have at our disposal, however, is imagination. And the wonderful thing is that the mind cannot tell the difference between 'virtual' and 'real' reality. Why do you think computer games are so successful?

Things you wish you'd done (or said): Over the Rainbow
Wealth Training Process

If it is no longer possible to do or say the thing you wish you'd done or said, do the following:

Say what you need to say in your mind's eye to the other person, or write a letter (which you can later burn). Do this in the same way as the previous processing. Speak until you have exhausted your words on the subject. Hear also, what the other person has to say and respond to that too. Once you are done, and the emotions have lifted, say 'It is finished'. Perform a symbolic act. Decide this is over.

If it's an act you wish you'd done, either do it in your mind's eye, write about it as if you are doing it, talk out loud to an imaginary friend telling them all about it, or use a substitute activity.

Doing things in the mind's eye is the same as speaking to someone in your mind's eye. Follow the previous processing on this, remembering to end when finished by saying 'It is finished' and to perform a symbolic act of completion.

You can use a substitute activity in many cases. Yes, you can substitute a twenty-year-old for that kiss . . .

Or you can help another child in need in place of the one you wish you had helped and didn't. Substitution works really well in the area of help. Especially if done with intention and attention. Say out loud, 'I do this act for Sam, whom I did not help when he asked me to all those years ago,' for example. You can also decide that though you may no longer be able to become a prima ballerina at fifty, you can (and will) take up ballroom dancing and excel at it. There are many things that can still be done, no matter how old you are. We hear of people in their seventies taking up skiing, or going to university to start a degree. It is never too late to become young again. Take that decision now.

You're never too old to fly

When I was in my late twenties I became bored with life and contemplated suicide. I had created and lost my first fortune; been married and divorced; owned a fancy house and cars; experienced wining and dining at the finest restaurants and had lavish holidays around the world in five star hotels. In short, I had done, in less than a decade what others do in a lifetime. What now, I thought? Do I start all over again? I felt too old to start anything, and I was only twenty-eight.

Then I met Martin, my wonderful Jungian mentor, and his studio filled with people doing the most amazing things. There were people of all ages, from their twenties to their sixties learning the piano, taking degrees, doing musicianship and voice training, learning new languages, while some also ran their own successful businesses or headed major corporations. It was truly an eye-opener.

234

Martin told me to create enormous goals, and that those goals would pull me into the future. He told me that it is I who will create the meaning in my life. He encouraged me to go back to my university studies and announced that I needed to pursue at least three PhDs. Martin taught me to look at the future in chunks of twenty and forty years. He told me of singers and musicians who began to do their best work in their sixties, seventies and nineties. Suddenly I was young again! I was only twenty-eight!

At Martin's studio I really came to understand that it is never too late to do anything, and I encourage you to grasp this concept with both hands. Imagine, for example, that it is twenty years from now and you are looking back on yourself as you are right at this very moment. What would you wish that you had done? (My editor is working on a first novel for a ninety-two-year-old!)

Now go out and do just that!

When you ask yourself 'what can I achieve in the next twenty years', you are plugging into a much more expansive range of possibilities. And in that range of possibilities, you may wish to take some of the things you wish you'd done and put them on a new 'to do' list for the future. Do that now. Take any of the things you wish you'd done, that you still want to do, and create a new 'to do' list. Celebrate that you have all the time in the world to achieve anything you want!

14

Relationships – Letting go the past:
Repairing the leaks

Where is your container leaking tears from the past?
Where is anger blocking your flow?

Things others have done or said: transforming the past

In the previous sections we looked at unfinished business in the area of relationships, where it involves what we have done to others. Now we will look at unfinished emotional business where it involves what others have done to us. This covers actual doing as well interactions with others which leave us feeling shrunk or diminished in some way. This may be a once-off occurrence or it may be an ongoing pattern with someone.

Sometimes something happens which makes us feel diminished in some way. We cannot explain it in words, but the feeling is there. It is similar to the vague undefined notions described in the section above, except here, whatever 'it' is, 'it' has been done to us.

When someone does or says something and we fail to express ourselves authentically, we also shrink a little. Every time we don't say what we really want to say, or don't do what we really want to do, we lose power.

And so we may, for many years after an event, keep replaying the event in our mind, yearning for a better conclusion. This creates blocks in our money flow, regardless of whether or not the event or person involved had anything to do with money. Everything is connected.

Also, where we have been emotionally hurt, we weep inside, drip, drip, drip, like a leaking tap. This leaks away precious energy, power, life force, and the energy of money flowing towards us. Which bring us to the subject of forgiveness, which is often easier said than done.

Forgiveness is a process of letting go of something that hurts, like removing a thorn from our side, or a splinter from our finger. There is no doubt that the thorn is a thorn. It is sharp and it hurts. We may never like it. There is no doubt that it hurt us. We cannot change that. We do not condone it. When we remove a thorn from our side, it is not with the aim of turning it into a sword, or singing its virtues, or understanding why it hurt us. No, when we remove a thorn from our side, it is primarily with the aim of letting go of something that hurts. It is with the objective of stopping the bleeding. We remove a thorn because it is taking our energy and our attention. We remove a thorn because we want to be whole.

It is in this spirit that we find the willingness to forgive. Those who speak of loving the person who hurt us are not walking around with a thorn in their side. First we remove the thorn, the rest may come later. Many people are so overwhelmed at the thought of loving someone who has done them great harm that they dare not remove the thorn. It is okay simply to remove the thorn, let go of the discomfort, release the blocked energy and transform the emotions. That is a great start, truly. The rest may come later on its own.

We will now look at people we have not forgiven, those who not only hurt us, but who now have the nerve to block our wealth flow with their presence, and draw our energy and attention back on to their memory day after day. We will rise up and remove these thorns from our side claiming back our power, our energy and our attention, and we will also complete the cycle by bringing it to completion.

'Don't you dare do that again, ever,' we will say, and they will hear us.

If someone throws you the ball, you don't have to catch it
Richard Carlson from *Don't sweat the small stuff . . . and it's all small*
stuff

Unfinished Emotional Business:
Letting go the thorns
Wealth Training Process

Please take careful note of the warning on processing under 'The Basics'. Do not process major trauma in these exercises. See a trained professional.

Do the following with compassion and without judgement. Set the clear intent of releasing energy blocks in your money flow caused by stuck emotions in the area of relationships.

You will need about an hour of uninterrupted time for this wealth training. You will need three large pieces of blank paper, A4 at least, preferably bigger.

Part One: Letting go the thorns
Wealth Training Process

1. First, invite the Divine to guard you as you do this processing.
2. Imagine a wall of protection around you which keeps all the emotions and energy you are dealing with here safely within the realms of Transformational Wealth Processing.
3. Create an imaginary circle within which the Transformational Wealth Processing will take place.
4. Make a list of all the people you have not forgiven, to a total of seven.

5. Do the following for each one, remembering not to process more than two people a day, and if they are really big thorns do only one at a time. Leave a few days in between.

6. Draw a border around a large piece of paper (A). Write the thorn's name on the top. Inside the border write all the things you think and feel and want to say to them and about them, and about this experience. Do not mince words. No one will read this. If you need to, use the other side of the paper too, also within a border. Write until you are finished, no matter how long this takes.

7. When you are finished underline important words and phrases in a different coloured pen and summarise into one sentence. Write this sentence on a separate piece of paper (B).

8. For two minutes, using words only, not sentences, list all the emotions you feel around this issue.

9. Underline the most important three. Write them down on paper B.

10. What would you most like to let go of in relation to this experience? Write for two minutes. Underline important words and phrases. Summarise into a sentence and write it on paper B.

11. What is the most important thing you feel you have lost, as a result of this experience? Write on this for two minutes.

12. When you are finished, underline important words and phrases in a different coloured pen and summarise into one sentence. Write this sentence on a separate, third, piece of paper (C).

13. How would you like to feel about this experience? Write for two minutes. Underline important words and phrases. Summarise into a sentence and write it on paper C.

14. How would you have liked this experience to have ended instead? Write for two minutes. Underline important words and phrases. Summarise into a sentence and write it on paper C.

15. What would you most like to regain if you could let go of this experience? Write for two minutes. Underline important words and phrases. Summarise into a sentence and write it on paper C.

Take a little three-minute break, but don't leave the energy of what you are doing – no chats, calls etc.

Part Two: Transforming the Energy
Advanced Wealth Transformation Process

You will need at least half an hour of uninterrupted quiet time for this part of the exercise. You cannot rush this exercise, so having extra time would be useful.

You have three pieces of paper
>   A – Facts and feelings around the thorny issue inside a border
>   B – How it was – Call this list OLD ENERGY
>   C – How you would like it to be – Call this NEW ENERGY

1. Sit on a comfortable chair at a table that can accommodate both the OLD ENERGY and the NEW ENERGY lists from the wealth training process above.
2. Focus your intent on transforming the energy around this person and event, as a means of repairing leaks and blocks in your money flow, thereby increasing wealth flow towards you.
3. Place the Old Energy list (B) on the table on the left, with list (A) underneath it.
4. Place the New Energy list (C) next to it on the right, with a gap between the two lists.
5. Enter a quiet and still place, using deep rhythmic breathing to still your body and mind.
6. Focus your intent on transforming the thought energy associated with the items on the old energy lists (A & B) into thought energy that will feed the items on your new energy list – that is, all the emotions, thoughts and feelings you listed.
7. Shut your eyes and be still.
8. State your intent that this work is done under the protection of the Divine and invite your image of the Divine to protect you while you do this work of energy transformation. Invite your image of the Divine to take a seat within your heart.
9. Imagine a warm fire burning between the two sets of lists. See it glowing in your mind's eye, and hear it crackle merrily.
10. Now imagine the thought energy from the words, feelings and emotions in the first, old list pouring into the fire as a column of

dark grey smoke. Use your breathing as you do this, and breathe the emotions out deeply into the fire. Breathe in and out through the heart.

11. Should you experience any physical or emotional discomfort, continue breathing out until the feeling is gone. This is important. Do not stop in the middle of such a process.

12. As the grey smoke pours into the fire it becomes clarified in a violet flame and emerges clear and golden, pouring into the New Energy list.

13. You breathe in this golden energy, through your heart, into every part of your body, as well as your mind, and fill yourself with the attitude and feeling of positive wealth flow.

14. When all the grey smoke has been transformed, take up the first list in your mind's eye and throw it into the fire.

15. Thank the fire and watch as it goes out and is gone.

16. Thank the Divine for the protection.

17. End the transformation by physically burning the old energy list (B) and the thorny issue list (A) in a safe way.

18. Wash your hands in a symbolic act of completion.

19. Absorb the good feelings that this process has initiated.

This is an extremely powerful energetic transformation. It is perfectly safe to do, if you follow the instructions closely and exactly. The most important thing to remember is to continue transforming the grey smoke, continue breathing out whatever emotion or physical discomfort arises into the fire until all the grey smoke, emotion, and discomfort is gone – no matter how long this takes.

Part Three: Releasing the Thorn
Wealth Training Process

1. Shut your eyes again and relax, using rhythmic breathing.

2. In your mind's eye see the thorn walking towards you from the distance.

3. See them sitting in front of you.

4. Say anything you wish to say to them, and hear their response.

5. Continue until you are finished.

6. If you are ready or able to forgive them, tell them so.

7. Let them know that you are finished with this cycle and have transformed the energy.
8. When you are done, watch as they walk away, until they are gone.
9. Decide this cycle is finished. Say it out loud and clap your hands three times.
10. Rejoice and celebrate!
11. Acknowledge that this process has opened up your wealth flows and cleared energetic debris from your life.
12. This is powerful processing. Take a break for a few days.
13. Prepare to receive.

After this exercise, expect to feel tired. Have a rest and take it easy. Apart from Grounding the New Energy (see below), do not continue with any other energetic transformational processes for at least a week, maybe even longer, depending on how you feel. Some of you may feel energised and elated – but even so, you should still take a break. Do not do any of the other transformational exercises (writing, drawing, reflecting) either until at least a week has gone by. But do, do the grounding below.

> *Imagine everyone is enlightened except you*
> Richard Carlson

Putting your money where your process is

It is always a good idea to ground any energetic transformation into the physical world. This can be seen as the planting of a seed, or utilising the good energy you have created in a tangible way. You do this by directing your intent through inspired action.

A great deal of energy was generated and redirected in your energetic templates in the previous exercises. By properly grounding this energy in the physical world, you help fulfil and develop the new emotions and attitudes you intend to cultivate. Through taking physical action in the world, you impress your intent upon the universe, and you imprint upon yourself the fact that what you are doing is a process of real, tangible wealth transformation. In effect, action is what sets the wheels of all intent and transformation rolling.

So, let us begin.

Part Four: Grounding the New Energy
Wealth Training Process

As soon as possible after doing the energetic transformation above, do
the following:

1. Think of something in your life that is important to do, resolve or
    act upon right now. This can be anything from the sale of an asset
    you may have been putting off, to applying for a job, starting a new
    business, or to asking for forgiveness. It is something that has been
    occupying your attention for some time, but that you have not had
    the time, energy, or resources to complete.
2. Put your intent on using the energy generated above for the success-
    ful completion of this task.
3. Perform the action with the full force of the energy now at your
    disposal.
4. Complete the task.
5. See this action as a symbolic act of grounding the energetic trans-
    formation and acting as new seeds that will sprout all the new
    attitude and feelings you have created.

Well done! Celebrate!

15

Unsuccessful Actions – Doing the things that work

Do your actions add power to your wealth flow?

Unsuccessful actions – do only the things that work

In this, the final part of transforming leaks and blocks, we will look at our daily actions in search of those unsuccessful actions which may be causing our container to leak constantly or even to become empty. This is an ongoing process of reflection that can greatly enhance everything you do. It is an ongoing search for excellence and a quest for raising your ceiling. It requires non-judgement and humility and, as always, the willingness to change.

We often perform actions, sometimes through habit, which may not be in alignment with our intent, and which may be producing unsuccessful results. Similarly, there are actions which we perform which produce excellent results, further our cause and help to strengthen our container. We need to know which actions to release and which to cultivate.

Sometimes our emotions provide the clues we need. Broadly speaking, if the way we go about doing something makes us feel stressed, anxious or uncomfortable, it may be time to consider doing whatever it is in a way which generates more uplifting emotions, and which will probably produce better results too.

I will give you a simple example. It has been my habit of many decades to thinly slice time with great exactitude. One of the reasons I do this is because I like to play with time, bending and stretching it to my will and intent. So I will, for example, give myself about fifteen minutes between getting up and leaving home, with shower, dress, make-up (minimal), breakfast (just tea and toast) and gathering what I need for the day (laptop, books, and so on) in between. I have done this successfully for many years. It has always worked for me, and I am never late – ever. Until, that is, little children entered the computation.

Little children have a hundred and one things they need to investigate and explore and 'dawdle' over, so that any step between 'a' and 'b' becomes a journey. Was I in the least bit daunted by this? Of course not. I hurried and shuffled and hissed at the poor little dears for quite a while before it occurred to me to change what I had been doing – successfully – for many years, which was no longer successful at all. I still don't get up in the early hours like many parents do, but my fifteen minutes has now trebled to three quarters of an hour to accommodate them. Had I not changed, I would probably have become a nervous wreck by now, and the poor littlies would have been in therapy!

Find out what you are doing that works, and what you are doing that doesn't. In some cases – in business, for example – you can accomplish a lot by merely asking your clients. Try to do something more than the standard 'how do you rate our service' form with squares for crosses which hospitals and hotels and garages provide. Try to talk to clients personally where you can – get direct input. If you want to see how your company performs, what works, become a client for a day, or get a close friend to do so. You will soon have all the answers you need. Simply pay attention.

And remember, just because you (or your industry) have been doing something in a certain way for the last twenty or fifty years does not mean that it is the only way it can be done. In fact, the longer you've been doing something the same way, the greater the likelihood that there is a much, much better way to do it. I totally believe that! (Of course this is another paradox! Because, yes, I do remember saying that if it's working, don't mess with it. And I believe that too.)

There is always a better way to do everything!
Kiki Theo

Seeing the Value of our Actions
Wealth Training Process

Spend a few days observing your actions, especially routine ones, and with a note on the emotions attached to each one. Set your intent on uncovering the actions which are successful and the ones that are not. After you have completed your observations (taking notes if you wish), do the following:

1. List all the actions you have observed, or can think of, that create stress and/or do not produce the results you want or need.
2. Identify the emotions and underlying assumptions for each one (for example, in my case, of rushing in the mornings, some of my assumptions were that the kids had to go at the same speed/pace as me, and that they were there to accommodate me).
3. Decide which of these actions you want to let go of and transform.
4. Create a new assumption, with new emotion, and new action that can give you the result and feeling you want for each one. (In my example my new assumptions were that it was in fact my job to accommodate the kids (not the other way round); that they did not need to keep pace with me. I did not want the stress of rushing them, and myself, and chose instead the emotion of ease and the feeling of containing them in a nourishing, playful 'motherhood-ness'.)
5. Execute your decisions.

6. Also discover, note and amplify those things that you do that produce results, and that enhance you and your container.
7. Celebrate! Rejoice! Acknowledge your achievements and transformation!

We are the hero of our own story
Mary McCarthy

16

A(nother) New Beginning

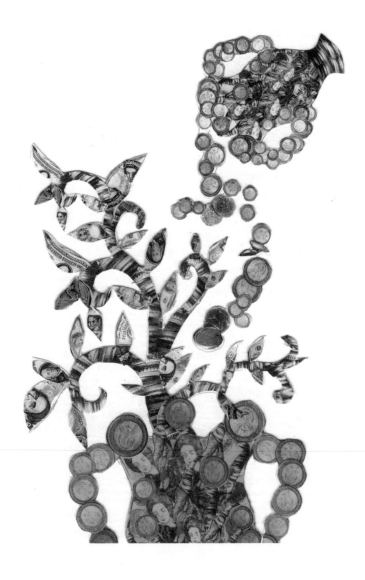

A(nother) new beginning

We are coming to the end of our journey, and the most important part – tying it all together. And this part, I will let you write :

- What has this book been all about? (*Send your answer of no more than 250 words into kiki@moneyalchemy.com and you stand to win a free one-on-one coaching session.*)
- What have you learnt that you can use in your day-to-day life?
- What have you transformed that will help increase your wealth flow?
- What is the condition of your container now?
- What more needs to be done?
- How will you contain your wealth?

Write an inspired action plan for where you go from here.

The 'Yet' has become the 'Now'

I have just finished editing and writing the tail end bits of this book. I was reading through and got to the second chapter, the section on container, the bit entitled Leaving the door of possibility open, or 'Yet' . . .

This is what I wrote there:

> *Being ready to receive is me, sitting here writing this, my second book, as a full-time 'occupation' having taken a sabbatical from delivering both money courses and business coaching to focus on writing, some six months ago. I sit here practising to be a fully fledged 'writer' when, to date, I have received something like nine rejections for the publication of my first book from various agents and publishers abroad. I sit here gamely telling you about my next book, book number three,* The Art of Conscious Manifestation, *when my first book is still not published. Yet. As things stand right now, you have not even read my first book. Yet. And it is the Yet which is the place of being ready to receive. It is the Yet which is the doorway into the future me – the published, best-selling author. It is the*

Yet which is that tentative ephemeral space of containing the dream.

But do you know that as I sit here writing, in my make-believe occupation as a make-believe author, to my make-believe audience, with input from time to time from my make-believe editor, having to stop in between for some make-believe signings of books and promotions around the world, do you know that you are sitting there also waiting for my book?

And do you know that as I sit here writing, there is no doubt in my mind that you will want to, and need to, and expect to read this book after you have read the first one! And I also absolutely know you will love the first one, which of course you will have read by the time you read this. All of this belief fits into that little space of Yet. So I write this for you. And as you are definitely real as you sit there reading this book, so then all this is real too.

And that, ladies and gentlemen, that is 'being ready to receive'. Definitely not something you can explain to Mum.

When I wrote that, I was sitting in my studio at home, holding the space for both *Money Alchemy* and this book to be published, but having no idea how it would happen. Now here I am, some eight months later, sitting in a recently acquired writing studio overlooking the little boats in Kalk Bay harbour, and not only have I just accepted an offer from Penguin for the publication of both books – but in the process I had to turn away three other publishers who also wanted the books!

Now, as I read through the book, as I read through what I wrote all that time ago, I am thrilled and amazed and humbled that this has all come together – just as I thought it would. And of course if it hadn't, you wouldn't want to read this book now, would you?

Thank you for sharing this journey with me! May your containers be solid and true! May wealth fill you with contentment, and may you know the true meaning of being rich!

The Wealth Journey – *soon at a bookstore near you* . . .

Of course I'm not going to just leave you here after all we've been through! The next book, which is actually almost finished (and is not *The Art of Conscious Creation* after all), is totally different from the last two, and it deals with wealth consciousness.

In ***The Wealth Journey***, an original model describing the dimensions of wealth and its creation from a psychological perspective, you will:

Discover the 9 Levels of Wealth Consciousness;
Confront the 9 Wealth Challenges;
Overcome the 9 Wealth Detours;
AND
Discover the 11 Secrets of Wealth Creation

Yes, there's a reason for all the nines, but I'm not telling – you have to read the book!

In ***The Wealth Journey*** we explore the dimensions of wealth consciousness not only in relation to 'where you are', 'where you are going', and 'how to get there', but also in terms of 'why you are *still* not there', and, most importantly, 'what to do once you are there'. Or, in the words of that chapter, 'Living the 9 "I"s of wealth'.

A truly inspiring adventure, no matter where you are on the path of wealth!

17

The Basics

How to use this book

The basics: how to use this book

1. This is a creative wealth training manual. Its purpose is wealth development and wealth expansion. Its aim is to transform you into someone who can contain more wealth. As you progress through the book you will uncover deeper and deeper layers of yourself. You will transform. You will become more, and therefore you will be able to contain more. Embrace this journey of becoming. Allow yourself to discover new aspects of yourself.

2. Do not allow the wealth training processing to stop you from reading further. Follow the instructions and simply reflect when you come to these sections, or follow any other instruction given at these points. You will still derive enormous benefit. Do go back, however, and complete the wealth training properly when you have time. You can do the processing as many times as you like, as each session will yield different results.

3. Before you start, ***set your intent.***
   An intent contains an implied commitment to, and a decision to act towards and achieve a want or desire. An intent is an act of focus and the application of will and action. So before you start reading this book, ***set your intent.*** *Do that now.*
   - Why are you reading this book? What are you hoping to learn, achieve?

- What would need to happen in your life for you to know this book has produced results?
- Be specific. Write a list if you need to.
- Be specific. What do you want? And what do you really want? What do you need, right now? It may have little to do with money. What are you trying to contain?
- Narrow down your list and pick what draws you the most at the moment. It does not really matter what it is, or whether it is logical. Don't make this too important.
- Be specific. Say: 'I want ....'. Then state this as an intent focused on containment.
- State your intention:
  I INTEND TO CONTAIN TWENTY MILLION IN MY TRUST ACCOUNT
  I INTEND TO EXPAND MY WEALTH CONTAINER TO CONTAIN A BIGGER HOME
  I INTEND TO CONTAIN A SUCCESSFUL AND PROFITABLE BUSINESS
  I INTEND TO CONTAIN AND MULTIPLY THE WEALTH I ALREADY HAVE

Do not create an intent out of negating something. Rephrase any negative want. For example, instead of 'I do not want to lose money' make it 'I intend to contain my wealth'. Don't make this big and heavy, or Very Important. Just create an intent which will act as beacon and goal and help you gain maximum benefit from reading this book.

4. How much benefit you receive from reading this book, how great a shift takes place in your life, how effortlessly you transform, how smoothly you increase your wealth, depends *on your decision* to do so, and doing the processing. *Allow* the transformation to take place. Allow your container to expand.
5. Decide now that this is a life-changing moment. Decide now that this is where your wealth makes a fast shift forward. Decide now that this book will change everything!
6. Are you ready?
   If not, what do you need to do to be ready? What do you need to let go of? What do you need to say 'no' to? What do you

need to say 'yes' to? Decide to do it. Do it. Do whatever you need to do to become ready for the expansion of your wealth.

7. Are you willing?
This is what real readiness is all about. Draw on your willingness to move forward and change. Draw on your willingness to go into the unknown and bring back the treasure.

8. Are you ready?

Alrighty then! Let's expand our wealth!

About the wealth training processes

The wealth training processes in this book are aimed at reconfiguring and reshaping you and your container. This work is intense and extremely powerful. You are literally re-patterning your resonance and reshaping your psyche. We do this by working on the levels below consciousness using the creative processes of free writing, drawing, symbolic acts, the use of metaphor, and clay work.

All of these methods are specifically used so as to reduce, as much as possible, interference from the left brain, logical mind. They are also aimed at accessing aspects of yourself which are below the tip of the iceberg. In other words, the processing will help you to discover things about yourself which are not normally in your conscious awareness.

Trust the process. You may not understand why you are doing some of the things you have been asked to do. Some of the tasks set may seem positively bizarre. Trust the process. The less you are able to rationalise what you are doing, the better. The wealth processing is part of a process. Trust the process and flow with it. This will symbolically release more wealth flow too.

There is no wrong way to do the wealth training. There is no wrong way to understand the prompts or questions. The prompts are open-ended for a reason. The prompts are 'vague' for a reason. Trust the process and believe that the way you understand and respond to these prompts is absolutely, exactly right for you at this time – because it is. On another day, when you repeat the training, you may understand and respond to a question in an entirely different way. The wealth training has been specifically designed to facilitate just that.

The processes we will be using for wealth training are creative processes using the right side of the brain – in other words, the creative side. For those of you who are unfamiliar with this type of work, allow yourself to enter new areas of possibility. Allow yourself to discover a new language. Yes, even serious business people in suits can do this type of processing, you do not need to be an artist or a 'creative' person. Everyone is creative. And wealth expansion is a very creative art.

- **Free writing**

Free writing is writing which allows whatever emerges to emerge on the pages. You do not think about what to write, how to phrase it, or worry about grammar or punctuation. You merely allow your hand to write. Again, it is setting your intent before the start which is key. The purpose behind all the writing is to discover the unknown, or the less obvious.

Gently remind yourself of this purpose before you begin to write. Keep it light, though.

Summarising whole paragraphs into one sentence at the end of an exercise after highlighting the most important parts may at first appear daunting, but it can be done. You are trying to get to the essence of what you are writing about. The summary does not need to be a logical conclusion derived from the sum total of your input. The summary is more a matter of asking yourself 'so what does all that really mean?' Or 'what is at the heart of all I wrote?' Again, allow the summary to surprise you.

Summarising in this way is also practice for honing your focus and intent. To create what you want you need to get specific, and you need to get to the point. Summarising practice helps you to do just that.

When doing the writing exercises:

○ Write for the recommended time only – use a timer.

○ Keep the pen moving, just write, don't think.

○ Do not censor anything – you can burn the paper later.

○ Begin with the prompt; if you become stuck, repeat the prompt.

- **Drawing**

Drawing is the same as free writing, except you are not using words, but marks on the paper. Allow what emerges to emerge without censoring or thinking. Once again, you are trying to discover the unknown about yourself, using yet another language. You do not need any artistic skill to do these exercises. Give yourself permission to observe what arises with interest.

You will be drawing your container and going back to it throughout the book, amending and changing as your reality changes. At the very end you may want to draw a brand new container.

○ Keep the crayons moving, just draw, don't think.

○ Do not censor anything – you can burn the paper later.

- **Symbolic acts**

A symbolic act can take the form of a specially created ceremony or it can be a mundane or routine activity which you perform with the intent to create change.

Some people call symbolic acts 'rituals'. 'Ceremony' is a better word. A ritual is a series of acts performed in exactly the same way every time – like, for example, the ritual of marriage, or christening a child. A ceremony may become a ritual for you if you repeat it regularly, in the same way.

A symbolic act is a way to focus your intent. It is a powerful means of concentrating and directing energy. The energy comes from your intent and from the act itself, and you are directing it towards a certain decision or outcome. Symbolic acts help us to pay attention. It is great to perform a ceremony at the start or end of something, as well as at a point of great change.

What you actually do in a symbolic act, is not as important as your focus and intent. What does matter, though, is that the symbolism you are using has relevance for you. For example, a snake has long been used as a symbol of healing and transformation by some. But for most people snakes are repulsive and to be feared. For those who fear snakes, a symbolic act for transformation that involved snakes as symbol would be counterproductive.

When you take a mundane activity and turn it into a symbolic act, you are setting up new patterns in the world around you and you are practising living those new patterns. It is like dress rehearsals before a play. So, for example, you may decide to clear out your wardrobe with the intent of letting go of that which no longer serves you in your life. It is the intent and focus that you set at the start that transforms the mundane act into a symbolic act of transformation. A mundane act carried out with the proper focus and intent can be likened to a meditation. Certainly it will create new pathways in your life in ways that appear to be quite miraculous.

- In ceremonies, use symbols that you can relate to.
- Whether performing a ceremony, or a mundane act, keep the symbolic act simple.
- Focus your attention and intent.
- Keep it light.

- **Working with symbol**

A symbol is that which represents something by virtue of association, thought, or similar qualities. A symbol is not the same as a sign, which is a literal representation. For example, white, lion, cross are symbols or purity, courage, Christianity. They are universal Western symbols. But symbol is also something very personal, different for everyone.

Words are the language of the rational and represent a certain type of thinking which is analytical, logical and realistic (unless you are free writing, that is). Symbol on the other hand is the language of a more creative type of thinking, intuitive, holistic, and deeply personal. When we integrate and align the two, we have much more creative potential at our disposal, much more energy and power.

Metaphor is the use of a word or description applied to something (an object or action, for example) which is not literal. Metaphor relates to transference (which is the literal Greek translation). With metaphor, we are transferring meaning, we are transferring ideas and beliefs, and ultimately we are transferring energy, because everything is energy.

Metaphor can be likened to symbol and is useful in expanding our perspective on life. We can take a situation which may be quite difficult to understand or relate to and radically transform it both in our minds and in reality by viewing it as metaphor for something else.

Metaphor and symbol can give meaning in situations that are hard to grasp. They can lighten heaviness and create a shift. Proper use of metaphor and symbol can create new pathways of thought and action, releasing energy that can be used for the creation of our dreams. Through the use of metaphor and symbol we can discover our innermost dreams and the means through which to attain them.

Throughout this book we will use the metaphor of a container for the transformation of self and the expansion of wealth. Enter into this metaphor and allow its secret language to unfold.

- **What to be aware of when doing creative wealth processing**

This is not a 'how to do' book. It's a 'how to become' book. This means change, and change is not always comfortable. The wealth processing may tire you. You will need time and space to integrate the shifts this work will initiate. All sorts of emotions and physical symptoms may arise. Mostly, these will pass, if you allow the space and time. As you release old ways of being and thinking, as you clear and reshape your container, your body may assist through the release of mucus – you may experience flu-like symptoms, or diarrhoea. This will pass.

Emotions may arise to be cleared. These are emotions that may be linked to the old patterns that you are releasing. You may feel angry, or depressed, or sad. These emotions too will pass, if you allow the time and space for this. Simply reminding yourself that this is part of the process of creating a better container for your wealth will be a great help to you at these times. It is also good to remind yourself of your intent for doing this work which you set at the start.

Whatever emotions arise, allow them to pass. Do not get attached to them, or involved with them. Do not try to analyse where they are from or how they got there. Simply observe them and allow them to pass.

There is only one exception to this. If, in the course of this processing, you find yourself being emotionally or mentally drawn into any traumatic event from your past, stop.

The purpose of this work is not to process traumatic events. Remind yourself of this before you start any of the wealth training processes. The purpose of the processing in this book is to cultivate your ability to contain more wealth.

Should you remember, or be reminded of some past trauma, please do not continue with the work that sparked this off. Stop. See a professional counsellor or therapist to deal with what has arisen before you continue. You can also skip to another section of work until you are able to see a professional.

This work will change you. It will change how you view money and the world, and it will change your ability and willingness to contain – not only wealth, but life itself.

This will surprise you, because the connection between the creative wealth training in this book and the creation of wealth itself will be a hard thing for your mind to grasp or understand – which is as it should be, after all. That's why it's called 'right brain processing'.

For some of the people who have done the *Money Well*™ training, there is a sudden or immediate improvement in their wealth – money starts to pour in, business expands rapidly, projects materialise. For others, it is a more gradual process of becoming. A subtle change that slowly seeps into every area of their life, so that one day they discover they are in a totally different place in their lives and wealth programme, with a radically different view of money and moneymaking than they had before.

Some of the changes this work will initiate have nothing to do with money. The *Money Well*™ training will facilitate the release of anything that does not serve you, if you allow it, and the opening up of brand new spaces and levels of being.

Tools you will need for wealth training processes

The wealth training processes you will be doing in this book require the following tools:
1. A large A4 Wealth Containing Book that you can write in.
2. A pen.
3. Several pieces of large, blank, poster cardboard paper – A3, white is best.
4. A box of nice crayons, pastels, coloured felt-tipped pens or coloured pencils, or the whole lot.
5. An egg timer, or other type of timing device.
6. No logic.
7. No seriousness.
8. No correction.
9. No censoring.
10. No one ever to look at what you have done, ever (unless you want it).
11. An open mind.

Give yourself time and space to do this work. Be aware that you may feel very tired after some of the processes. Take time to rest. Take time to integrate the shifts and changes.

Reflection

One of the most important aspects of any of these exercises is to reflect at the end.

That is not the same as analysing, psychoanalysing (even worse) or judging (worse still!).

Analysing is when your mind either tries to make sense of the situation, like 'how can I not contain my body?' or when it tries to overcompensate by reaching profound conclusions like 'this must be a metaphor for when I am beside myself'.

Psychoanalysing is when the mind does the above, wearing a psychologist's hat, like 'I have been beside myself ever since my mother took away my bottle at age three'.

Judging is when you blame yourself (which can be done with or without the above) like 'she took away my bottle because I ate

260

too much, I still eat too much and that is why I am beside myself, because I can't fit into myself! I need to go on a diet!' None of these methods are useful. None is reflection.

Reflecting is allowing information to wash over you. You just observe what is. You look at what is there, with an open and enquiring attitude, ready to discover something new, ready to be surprised. Whereas analysing is an event – it happens here and now, straight away – reflection is a process and takes place over time. Allow time for the new to emerge.

Keep it light

The most important requirement for this work is a light touch. Keep it light. Keep it fun. Keep it magical. Keep focused on the light. And trust the process.

In conclusion

1. To derive maximum use from this book state your specific intent for what you want to achieve at the start of the book and of every wealth training.
2. Do the wealth processing lightly, with attention and intention.
3. There is no wrong way to do the wealth processes. There is no wrong way to understand the instructions.
4. When you free write or draw, allow undiscovered aspects of yourself and the subject you are exploring to emerge without censorship.
5. When you are performing a symbolic act, use symbols that have meaning for you and keep it simple.
6. Trust the process. Trust that it will produce the results you want.

Keep it light, and have fun!
Good Luck!

18

My Story

To tell you about my story would take a very long time. I have lived long and fast. I have lived many lives. On my website *www.moneyalchemy.com* you can read both a fairy tale version of my tale, and an extract from the *Money Alchemy* book which includes my biography.

In a nutshell, you have an ordinary girl from humble beginnings who had a traumatic childhood and grand aspirations to make the world a better place; making her way through the world of business, transformation, life and love; with many ups and downs, failures and success, joys and pain, and profound revelations; to a grand finale of 'retiring' at thirty-nine and a new beginning in a beach house with a loving husband and two beautiful children. Then she teaches and writes books about wealth creation – to make the world a better place.

It's the story of many people. Many people, like myself, have turned humble beginnings into success, transcended trauma and misfortune, started and grown businesses from the grass roots up, and learnt many valuable lessons about life, business and money-making along the way. But very few write about it and even fewer create a workable means for others to do the same.

My unusual combination of successful business experience in a variety of fields, and extensive background in the field of transformation, makes this book and approach unique. But ultimately this book is not about me, it's about you. It's about what you will allow to be awakened within you. It's about your openness to your wealth expansion journey and to the next step in your path. It's about your willingness to change.

My story is your story. It's a story of change and transformation. It's a story of growth and expansion of self. And when we expand, everything around us expands too. That's what *The Money Well*™ story is all about.

Acknowledgements

There are many people I would like to thank for helping me arrive at this point in my life:

My father, for leaving the doors of possibility open; my mother who helped me discover my inner strength and taught me the love of books; Martin de Chatillon, wonderful teacher and mentor who introduced me to Jung, working with symbol, and who said that I should write; Allegra Taylor at Skyros who encouraged my writing further; Anthony Prolad who put me on the path; Mr Au my first tai-chi teacher who taught me about energy; Rob Nairn, of the Kagyu lineage of Tibetan Buddhism, beloved teacher of meditation, who taught me how to work with the mind; the staff, teachers and participants of Skyros Holistic Holidays for facilitating a major shift (and providing a husband); Craig Wilkie, my fabulous business partner without equal, who has shared most of my wealth creation moments, and who was there from the beginning; Anne Schuster who has helped me hone my writing skills, and for the women's monthly writing group, for keeping the writing faith through the years; all my clients and staff across time for their trust and support; and all the participants of the Money Alchemy courses as well as coaching and corporate clients for their courage and for trusting me to facilitate their journey. Thank you to everyone at Penguin for their trust, for indulging ample author's input, and for their commitment to creating a superior product. Special thanks to Louise Grantham, Alison Lowry and Reneé Naudé! Finally I would like to thank Alex and Sasha, the joys of my life, who teach me daily the great art of motherhood, and the love of my life Shaun, who holds the space for me to transcend, I love you.

A special thanks to Divine Spirit for protection, guidance, and a wonderful sense of humour!

Copyright acknowledgements

'Jump off the Edge' poem is reproduced with permission from *Writing the Self: An Anthology of Women's Writing* – (Women's Writing Workshop, 2008)

Bibliography

I acknowledge the following books which have helped me shape my transformational processes:

Life Choices, Life Changes: The Art of Developing Personal Vision through Imagework – Dina Glouberman (Thorsons – Harper Collins, 1999)

The Tibetan Art of Positive Thinking – Christopher Hansard (Hodder Mobius, 2003)

Recommended Reading

The following books will be helpful to you on your wealth transformation journey:

Transforming Wealth Consciousness
Money Alchemy: Into Wealth & Beyond – Kiki Theo (Penguin Books, 2008)

The Process of Creation and Manifestation
The Power of Intention: Learning to Co-create Your World Your Way – Dr Wayne W Dyer (Hay House, 2004)

Excuse Me, Your Life is Waiting: The Astonishing Power of Feelings – Lynn Grabhorn (Hampton Roads Publishing Co. Inc., 2003)

Transforming Self
The Secret of the Shadow: The Power of Owning Your Whole Story – Debbie Ford (Hodder Mobius, 2005)

The Alchemy of the Heart – Reshad Feild (Element Books Ltd, 1990)

Transforming Mind
Tranquil Mind: Introduction to Buddhism and Meditation – Rob Nairn (Kairon Press, 2004)

Diamond Mind: A Psychology of Meditation – Rob Nairn (Kairon Press, 2001)

The Tibetan Art of Serenity: How to Heal Fear and Gain Contentment – Christopher Hansard (Hodder Mobius, 2008)

Transformational Processing
Life Choices, Life Changes – The Art of Developing Personal Vision through Imagework – Dina Glouberman (Thorsons – Harper Collins, 1999)
The Tibetan Art of Positive Thinking – Christopher Hansard (Hodder Mobius, 2003)
Taming the Tiger – Dharma-Arya Akong Rinpoche (Dzalendara Publishing, 1987)

Principles of Success
The Dip – The extraordinary benefits of knowing when to quit (and when to stick) – Seth Godin (Piatkus, 2007)
The Greatest Salesman in the World – Og Mandino (Bantam Books, 1995)
(All the principle for success, sales, marketing, and wealth creation are contained in this very small, very old book – a classic must read.)

Other
The Art of Power – Thich Nhat Hanh (Harper Collins, 2007)
Pathways to Bliss: Mythology and Personal Transformation – Joseph Campbell (New World Library, 2004)
A Little Book on The Human Shadow – Robert Bly (Element Books Ltd, 1992)

For courses and seminars see www.moneyalchemy.com and www.moneywell.co.za

Guided energetic transformations found in this book (and more) are available on The Money Well™ Processing CD available on these websites.

I dedicate the merit of this work to our enlightenment and the enlightenment of all beings.